Praise for *Brilliant Email*

Brilliant Email has revolutionised my life, by telling me simply how to control and manage my email. It is a must read for over-loaded emailers!

Professor Cary L. Cooper, Lancaster University Management School

Monica's book has something for everybody; a jargon-free, pragmatic and effective approach to communicating brilliantly using email.

Mike Southon, Financial Times *columnist and best-selling business author*

This book is clear and easy to follow and the next best thing to having Monica sitting next you giving practical hints and tips ... She not only clearly identifies the issues we all face but also offers a range of easily implemented solutions.

Rachel Oliphant, Senior Associate, Risk & Knowledge Management, McGrigors LLP

If there's anything you want to know about email and getting the best out of it, Monica knows the answer ... This book is a really good reference point for people who want to tame their email addiction and improve their skills.

Tim Allen, Business Systems Manager, Balfour Beatty Rail Infrastructure

If only half the book's advice were put in to practice in organisations, it would make a positive impact on corporate image and employee effectiveness.

Karen Dunn, Head of Retail Learning at EON UK

With *Brilliant Email* Monica has created a unique reference book for email users, which combines a *Haynes Manual* and *Debrett's*. This book will appeal to every strata of the business world.

Jerry Stimpson, General Manager, Crown Closures UK

email

How to win back time and increase your productivity

Monica Seeley

Prentice Hall
is an imprint of

Harlow, England • London • New York • Boston • San Francisco • Toronto • Sydney • Singapore • Hong Kong
Tokyo • Seoul • Taipei • New Delhi • Cape Town • Madrid • Mexico City • Amsterdam • Munich • Paris • Milan

PEARSON EDUCATION LIMITED

Edinburgh Gate
Harlow CM20 2JE
Tel: +44 (0)1279 623623
Fax: +44 (0)1279 431059
Website: www.pearsoned.co.uk

First published in Great Britain in 2011

© Pearson Education Limited 2011

The right of Monica Seeley to be identified as author of this work has been
asserted by her in accordance with the Copyright, Designs and Patents Act 1988.

Pearson Education is not responsible for the content of third party internet sites.

ISBN: 978-0-273-74255-5

British Library Cataloguing-in-Publication Data
A catalogue record for this book is available from the British Library

Library of Congress Cataloging-in-Publication Data
Seeley, Monica.
 Brilliant email : how to win back time and take control of your inbox
/ Monica Seeley.
   p. cm.
 ISBN 978-0-273-74255-5 (pbk.)
  1. Electronic mail systems--Management. 2.   Office mail
 procedures--Management.   I. Title.
 HE7551.S427 2011
 651.8'4692--dc22
                                2010037611

Microsoft screenshots reprinted with permission from Microsoft Corporation.

10 9 8 7 6 5 4 3 2 1
14 13 12 11 10

Typeset in 10/14pt Plantin Regular by 3
Printed and bound in Great Britain by Henry Ling Ltd, at the Dorset Press,
Dorchester, Dorset

This book is dedicated to Angela Peach, Lorna Campbell and Susan Oakes. Thank you for your support over the years with the business and for being my judges, jury, unpaid researchers – and even guinea pigs – in my quest to find the most effective and productive ways of using email.

Contents

About the author

In 1989 I founded Mesmo Consultancy (www.mesmo.co.uk) to coach executives and organisations in how to use IT to improve personal and business productivity. At that time this meant using computers and software primarily to create documents and analyse data. It was rarely about communication, as email was still the exception rather than the rule. Today, things are reversed and I specialise in enabling people to improve their productivity and communications by managing their email more effectively. Typically this saves them at least 45 minutes every day.

My clients are drawn from a wide range of roles (from CEOs to PAs), sectors and size of businesses across the UK and Europe. I work with them through workshops, one-to-one coaching and consultancy. Many organisations use my expertise to help them create and implement a business-wide email best practice strategy, guidelines and Acceptable User Policies (AUPs).

As a Senior Visiting Fellow at Sir John Cass Business School, City University, my research includes the future of email and the use of social networking tools to gain sustainable business benefits.

Until 2008 I was author of *The Times*' column, 'PC Stress Busters'. I have contributed to and written several books, including *Managing in the Email Office*. As the 'EmailDoctor' on Twitter I post daily tips on smart email management.

Living in Dorset, I am on the Dorset Chamber of Commerce and Industry and chair its digital taskforce, championing fast broadband across the county.

Outside of my working life, my great loves are golf, classical music and a black and white cat called Bessie.

Acknowledgements

No man is an island.
John Donne

I would like to offer my gratitude and appreciation to all those at Pearson who have supported me while writing this book. Special thanks go to Samantha Jackson and her team for their patience and nurturing of this project, and to Richard Stagg for encouraging me to write the initial proposal.

Thank you to all my clients and colleagues who have given me permission to use examples of their emails to illustrate best practice – whether by name or anonymously. I am also most grateful to Lucy Kellaway for making the time for me to interview her as an example of how your mailbox is really just a DNA fingerprint of you.

My thanks go to all those who have contributed supporting information and material and given of their time so generously, especially Peter Bauer of Mimecast, Ed Brill at IBM, Graham Cluley at Sophos, Gary Marsh and Mark Hamilton at KPMG, Michael Osterman at Osterman Research, and Jonathan Spira at Basex.

Thanks to Lorna Campbell for being an excellent wordsmith and helping me turn my draft material into more eloquent prose, and also to Rachel Hayter and Rhian McKay.

To all the friends who have suffered my late arrival, whether for a drink or game of golf, I thank you for your understanding.

Introduction

Man is still the most extraordinary computer of all.

John F. Kennedy

Email – saviour or timewaster?

Take a cool detached look at your inbox and ask yourself, do you really need all that email? Sixty-six per cent of people I work with tell me they only need between 25–75 per cent of what they receive. Now ask yourself:

- Do you receive too much email? Most people will say yes.
- Do you send too much? Most people don't think they do.

Where has all this email come from? And how much time (and natural resources) is being wasted by all this unnecessary email? My work and research reveals that most people waste about 21 working days per year (half a day a week) simply dealing with unwanted emails. Add to this time wasted reading and re-reading emails which are poorly written, hunting for emails, replying when not necessary and the time soon mounts up. Little wonder many now consider email to be one of the major drains of personal and business productivity and drivers of the long-hours culture.

Yet email can be a timesaver, improve efficiency, help drive up business, save time by bridging time and location differences and much more.

A free hour, every working day of your life

If you could create a free hour in every working day of your life, what would you do with it? A recent survey I conducted to find out how people would spend this extra time revealed that none of their top three priorities involved getting closer to their email. They were:

- Going out for a 'proper lunch' with a business colleague or client.
- Doing some exercise such as a brisk walk, yoga, or a jog (or, in joint second place, planning a client-site visit).
- Going and chatting to a colleague.

liberate yourself from your mailbox

The answer to finding that extra hour is to liberate yourself from your mailbox.

This book will show you ways to save time dealing with your inbox by:

- reducing the volume of emails you need to handle each day
- tackling any latent email addiction and dependency
- choosing and using alternatives to email to save time
- writing emails that result in fewer rounds of email ping-pong
- managing your use of attachments
- staying the right side of the laws and regulations relating to email.

Use email as intended

The first email was sent in 1971 by Ray Tomlinson, an American computer scientist. Ray invented email as a system to send simple messages when sending files to colleagues (for example, short exchanges regarding content and any special lines of code or possible problems with it). Currently, it is used in various forms, from one-word messages to three-page letters with attachments.

To create brilliant email, you first need to check that it is the best and most appropriate method to communicate. Too many emails these days are unwanted or inappropriate communications.

Exponential growth in email volumes

Today email dominates most business people's lives. According to the leading technology market place analysts, the volume of emails sent per day worldwide (excluding spam) is around 200 to 250 billion messages.

My data and that of others suggests that most people now spend about three hours a day dealing with email. This begs the questions:

- What happens to the real day job – for example, selling, writing, managing a team, processing the accounts – while you are dealing with all that email?
- Is the working day becoming longer to enable us to cope with email?

Can I manage my mailboxes more efficiently to save time?

By being more focused and adopting some basic rules, it is very easy to reclaim most of that lost time, create a shorter working day and have a little more 'me' time – providing you have willpower.

My early work coaching executives to use IT to improve their personal productivity quickly demonstrated that effective use of technology does not depend on knowing which buttons to press.

It helps, but more crucial is knowing what you want to achieve and appreciating your own strengths and weaknesses.

Your inbox is a DNA fingerprint of you and your *modus operandi*

How much email time you can save depends on you, your approach to work and the culture of your organisation. Your inbox is a DNA fingerprint of you. The amount of email you receive will also depend on a number of factors, including your:

- **role** – front-line, back-office, senior, junior, etc.
- **information needs** – whether you like to collect lots of information or be very selective
- **personality** – tidy, unruly, introvert, extrovert, etc.
- **management style** – (both yours and that of *your* manager) empowering, micro management, etc.

Lucy Kellaway and her taste for 'controlled' chaos

Here is a glimpse into one person's mailbox, which underpins the proposition that your mailbox is a DNA fingerprint of you.

In September 2003 I met and coached Lucy Kellaway (the *Financial Times* columnist, author of the 'Martin Lukes' column, *Who Moved My BlackBerry?* and *In Office Hours*). Lucy had papers and books everywhere and, yes, you guessed, all her emails just sat in her inbox. The thought of filing them away after she had read them was anathema to her.

Lucy Kellaway afterwards wrote in the *Financial Times*:

After she [Monica] had gone I spent a satisfying hour or three doing exactly what she had told me: shifting emails into folders … I felt all clean and tidy, and vowed I would stay that way forever. Monica referred to my poor organisation of emails, but said this reflected my personal modus operandi.

She [Monica] was spot-on here. It is precisely because of my personal modus operandi that the very next day I had reverted to my bad old ways. However much I would like to have a tidy inbox, it simply is not the way I work.

It is just the same with my desk. Every six months I have a big clear out and chuck everything away. I like it clean but I can't keep it that way. I seldom do piles and never do files.

Has she changed in the light of a mounting volume of emails, which reflect her rise in popularity and her new roles, including a non-executive directorship? In June 2010 I re-interviewed Lucy:

No, I haven't changed, I still make no attempt to manage my email, because it works for me. When I come in I mark all my emails for deletion, then scan them and unmark those I need to keep, for example, readers' comments, emails from colleagues. The urgent ones are replied to and if I don't feel like doing email (usually because there is a column to write), I leave the non-urgent ones and do them in a batch later on.

Lucy is a self-confessed 'email junkie', always checking her email. 'I love to send email and even send to colleagues nearby as "a discrete running commentary on an office incident".' This reflects her profession as a leading writer on office politics. Lucy may not be the best role model for effective use of email. Nonetheless, while she does not (and probably never will) folder her emails, as the volume of emails has risen she has become more discerning and focused about how and when she replies to the non-critical emails. She had adapted her use of email to suit her *modus operandi*.

You too must be selective and find ways of dealing with email which you feel will work for you and your business. There are no absolutes, only good guidelines and best practice. I will show you how to play to your personal strengths and overcome your weaknesses as an email user in order to be more productive.

Getting the most from this book

Before you start

To make the most of your investment in this book, take a minute to ask yourself the following questions:

- What annoys me most about email (mine and others) and do I want to fix it?
- What aspects of my use of email do I most want to improve?

For example, if timesaving is your key goal (and it is for most of us), you should know that putting recipients' names in the right box ('To' or 'Cc') will immediately save you 15 minutes a day. (If you are in a hurry to know more, go straight to Chapter 11 for more information.)

Brilliant tips

Brilliant Email is packed with practical tips and hints. They are drawn from the experiences of the many 'brilliant' clients and colleagues with whom I have had the honour and pleasure of knowing, both in business and socially.

Five steps

As the chart opposite shows, there are five steps to taking personal control of your mailbox and saving yourself at least an hour a day.

Each part of the book focuses on one of these five steps. You can either work through each step, or just dive in and deal with the area you feel currently causes you most grief and achieve quick

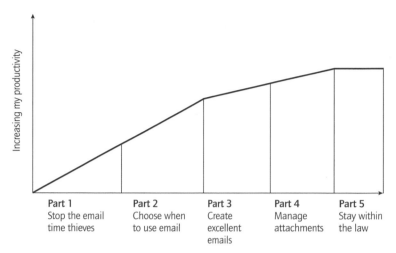

Five steps to improving my productivity

gains. Here are some typical issues you may want to address which will give you an idea of where to start.

Part 1: Stop the email time thieves

- Do you want to reduce the volume of unnecessary email?
- Would you like to be able to find emails more quickly?

Part 2: Communicate more effectively by choosing and using the right channel

- Do you ever get the gnawing feeling that there might be a smarter way to work and communicate?
- Do you want to know quicker ways to get repetitive tasks done? (For example, arranging meetings, finishing reports.)

Part 3: Create excellent emails

- How often do you send an email that does not receive a response?
- Do you send emails and find everyone – even those in the 'Cc' box – reply?

Part 4: Managing attachments for extra efficiency

- Are you always over your mailbox limit?
- What's the smartest way to send multiple attachments?

Part 5: Stay the right side of the law

- Do you know if your email would stand up in court if there was a problem?
- How do you spot when an email is spam or contains a virus?

Alternatively you can read through all the tips and *selectively* pick and try those that you feel will work for you. Selectively – not because all the content is not equally good, but rather because we are human and we all have our own preferred way of working (as illustrated by my interview with Lucy Kellaway on pages xvi–xvii).

Using your email software to best advantage

At a personal level, improving your own productivity is about 70 per cent about managing yourself and 30 per cent knowing how to use your email software to help you. There is a multitude of email software in use, including Outlook, Notes, GroupWise, Thunderbird, Google, Hotmail and Entourage (for Mac users), and each version has its own quirks.

In this book we highlight how to use Microsoft Outlook 2007 (as it is the most dominant system), and occasionally Notes and Entourage. If you use another software system and you spot a function you like, just search your 'Help' function or on the web to see if and how it can be done in the software *you* use.

Terminology – mailbox or inbox

In this book, 'mailbox' is used to mean all your email folders, including 'Deleted' and 'Sent' items. 'Inbox' refers to only the folder for your new emails: i.e. the one you most commonly see when you open your email software and from which hang your other folders ('Sent', 'Action pending', etc.).

Other supporting resources

To make *Brilliant Email* as useful and easy to find your way around as possible there are the following features:

- **Brilliant tips** – top-level tips to save time.

- **Brilliant examples** – to highlight the benefits of adopting the best practice and the pitfalls of taking the wrong approach.

- **Brilliant timesavers** – to help you save time and work more efficiently.

- **Brilliant dos and don'ts** – to remind you of what to do and what not to do.

- **Brilliant definitions** – key words and phrases that you need to know about.

- **Brilliant recaps** – quick reference guides at the end of each chapter.

www.brilliant-email.com

To accompany this book, I have created a new website called www.brilliant-email.com. This contains more tips and hints, disaster stories, results of surveys, useful links and online benchmarking tools (such as an 'Outlook IT Fitness Check' and 'Email Clarity' tool).

You can also register for a free monthly 'ebriefing' newsletter with further tips and hints and details of forthcoming workshops and events. Alternatively, simply send an email to: information@brilliant-email.com.

You can also follow me on Twitter as the 'EmailDoctor' and join my Facebook site and become an 'EmailDoctor' fan.

Lastly, if you have any questions or any tips you would like to share with other readers, I'd love to hear from you. You can email me at information@brilliant-email.com.

To start seeing what the best people do brilliantly in order to save time (often at least an hour a day) dealing with their email, read on.

PART 1

Stop the email time thieves

'Time is the scarcest resource and unless it is managed, nothing else can be managed.'

Peter Drucker

A new email takes on a life and priority of its own. We have been conditioned to check our email continually and respond instantly to new message alerts. We save every email 'just in case', and hence require ever larger mailboxes and servers.

Five questions that recur regularly when talking to clients and running workshops are:

- How often do I really need to check my emails?
- How long can I leave an email before responding?
- Is it acceptable to switch off my mobile email device (BlackBerry and iPhone, etc.), when I am out of the office, particularly when on leave?
- What's the best way to store and organise my mailbox?
- How can I stay within my mailbox size limit?

Constantly checking your email is probably the number one time thief, making us less productive and increasingly stressed. In 2005 a study sponsored by Hewlett-Packard found that constantly dipping in and out of your inbox can diminish your IQ by up to ten points. This is twice the impact inflicted by taking drugs such as marijuana for a prolonged period of time. Why? Because constant interruptions stop us thinking strategically and re-programme our brains to think only tactically. This is not a good idea if your job requires a high level of strategic thinking.

Spira and Goldes (in their report 'Information overload: we have met the enemy and he is us') estimated that constant interruptions of taking phone calls and checking emails cost American business a staggering $650 million per year. They estimated that the average knowledge worker (such as banker, lawyer, journalist) lost 2.1 hours a day due to interruptions. In addition, many studies have now shown that multitasking is not as productive as we like to imagine. For a good review of the growing evidence in favour of focused behaviour see Maggie Jackson's book *The Erosion of Attention and the Coming Dark Age* and John Freeman's *The Tyranny of E-mail.*

Interruptions by new email alerts add, on average, five to fifteen minutes to each task we do. Why? Because each time we stop, it takes us time to recover and retrace our steps.

What would happen if you didn't look at your emails for an hour? As senders, we all think our email is the most urgent. As recipients, we feel we have to deal with each new email as it arrives. But, of course, this isn't true.

As the volume of emails grows, so too does the amount of storage space needed. Current estimates suggest that users like you and I generate about 12 MB of emails per day. The larger the mailbox, the longer it takes to find an email, even with the fastest search engine.

The first step may be the hardest but it will reap the quickest rewards

The first and most important step towards being more productive is to prioritise your time and your information requirements.

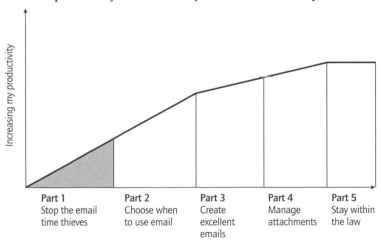

Five steps to improving my productivity – stop the email time thieves

Part 1 of this book addresses the fundamental challenges of saving time and keeping control of your mailbox while:

- limiting the number of times you check your emails
- decreasing the number of emails you need to handle each day
- ensuring that every email that warrants a reply receives one
- taking time out from email when on leave
- reducing email addiction and dependency as appropriate.

CHAPTER 1

Take control – stop email dominating your day

He who controls others may be powerful, but he who has mastered himself is mightier still.

Lao Tsu

I n this chapter we focus on how to deal with your inbox more effectively so that you get more done. You'll find out how to take control of your email and thus avoid being dominated by it.

Specifically, you will learn to save time by:

- managing your time at the inbox during the day
- avoiding time thieves such as new email alerts and unwanted email
- managing the recipient's expectations and time
- dealing constructively with new emails (the 'Four Ds' – Deal, Delete, Delegate or Defer).

Cast your mind back to the last time you were doing something important and you stopped to look at an incoming email. What happened? Probably dealing with both the first task and the email took longer, and if a second email popped up in the meantime, neither of the first tasks would have been completed properly.

Most research concludes that the optimum time for focusing on one task is 45 minutes. After that, a two- or three-minute break improves our productivity. This is the opposite of allowing ourselves to be interrupted. So let's look at how you can regain control of your day, your task list and your life, and rule your mailbox rather than it ruling you.

How often should you check your email?

To some extent it depends on your role. Here are some options that work well for many people. Only check your emails either:

- three/four times a day (for example, in the morning, after lunch and in the late afternoon)
- every hour
- once a day (preferably at the end).

There will always be exceptions, such as playing email ping-pong when working with someone to complete a project or waiting for some information. For others in front-line services, work comes by email and they may need to check more often. However, most of the time you must ignore new email and concentrate on the report, presentation, budget or task in hand.

 **tip**

Try to limit the number of times you check your email to a maximum of five times a day.

Leave checking your email until mid-morning

We have all had important tasks that need completing by mid-morning (a presentation, proposal or press release to draft, an essay to write, CVs to review, etc.). You have all the information, yet still you are tempted to check your emails before you start. Well, don't. Get started on your number one priority before you do anything else.

Timothy Ferriss, author of *The 4-Hour Work Week* says, 'Never check your emails first thing in the morning. Instead complete your most important task to avoid using lunch or reading emails as a postponement excuse.' Someone will soon come to find you if they really need you urgently.

brilliant timesaver

Switch off all those distracting new email alerts (from the 'ping' sound to the floating box). You will be amazed at how much more quickly you finish the task in hand.

In Microsoft Outlook, go to 'Tools/Options'. From the 'Preferences' tab, click on 'E-mail Options/Advanced E-mail Options' and deselect (un-tick) all the boxes in the pane marked 'When new items arrive in my inbox' (Figure 1.1).

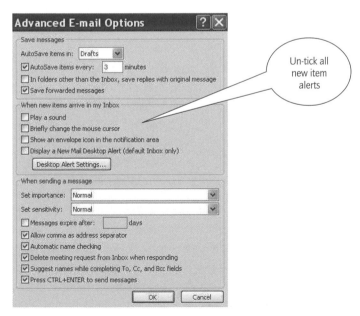

Figure 1.1 Turning off new email alerts in Microsoft Outlook

Managing response expectations

How do you react when someone demands an instant response? Do you think it is reasonable to expect an instant reply to your emails? Many questions often need a substantive response requiring careful consideration and additional information. This is a constant problem, especially for lawyers and accountants. One lawyer told me how, in the middle of a frenetic takeover, a client who was actually in their offices emailed her a question and shortly afterwards walked to her desk to see why she hadn't responded straightaway.

Furthermore, there are always those urgent emails which, it seems, cannot wait. PAs often say that emails need instant attention when 'The boss wants their coffee', 'The client expects an instant reply', 'My manager expects me to keep an eye on their inbox', and so on.

Educate others to wait, establish a sensible response time

Don't succumb to this drive for instant communication; establish priorities and set expectations.

One PA I met adopted the principle of checking her emails fewer times in the day. As a result, her manager soon started to pop out to ask her if she had read the email he had just sent. She explained what she was doing in order to work more efficiently and 'get the day job done'. They agreed that he would speak/call when something was really urgent.

> don't succumb to this drive for instant communication

For many PAs, this expectation of being chained to the mailbox is a real issue and one that needs to be addressed. Ask your manager what their priorities are. Many do not realise what is going on because the topic is never really talked about. Suggest that your manager talks to you or uses the phone to alert you to urgent matters, rather than relying on you checking your email every few seconds.

You could argue that constantly phoning is just as disruptive, but people rarely phone every few seconds. More importantly, it is about ring-fencing your time (even if it's only for half an hour) in order to concentrate and deal with the matter in hand, rather than feeling that you are constantly on call. It is the latter that is so disruptive and stressful.

Start by deciding what a reasonable response time is. Next, set up an out-of-office message to acknowledge messages and communicate when you will be able to reply. Then tell the people you work closely with that you won't be constantly online and explain why.

brilliant tip

Set up an out-of-office message (auto-reply) for all emails, thanking the sender for their message and telling them you expect to be able to reply at such and such a time.

Those who work in front-line support roles, where an immediate response is needed (for example, helpdesks, travel advisors, doctor), can still apply an out-of-office message, but give a shorter response time. This is the equivalent to an engaged sound on a phone.

We must be realistic recipients and senders; we can only deal effectively with one task at a time. Chapter 5 covers establishing sensible response times in more details.

A lawyer, when he needs quiet time, uses this message:

'I am away from the office today. If your email is urgent, please call my assistant Sue on telephone number ... or email ... Otherwise I will deal with your message on my return.'

From time to time during the day he checks his messages and replies to key clients. In this way he exceeds expectations and creates customer satisfaction.

By managing senders' expectations, you gain time and space to reply and prioritise your work. Ferriss calls this approach 'Beg forgiveness; don't ask permission' and, like the lawyer quoted in the example above, finds it works wonders once people realise it's a win-win situation. We all become less stressed and frustrated once expectations are managed.

Clearly some people might not be happy – your boss, for example. But in such a situation, be bold, and ask them to prioritise your work. Is it email, email and more email they want from you or would they like you to complete that important proposal, see a customer, attend a meeting, etc.?

How to save time dealing with your inbox

Employ thy time well if though meanest to get leisure.

Benjamin Franklin

With all these emails sitting in your inbox, how can you ensure each email is answered properly, within a sensible timeframe and that nothing slips through? Furthermore, how can you avoid opening and re-opening each email to remind yourself about its content? Lastly, how can you save time dealing with the flow of new email traffic? Read on ...

 **brilliant** tip

Handle each email once and once only. Whenever possible, avoid cherry picking and flicking your way through the list of emails in your inbox.

Re-reading emails can be very costly to your time and business productivity. Back in 2000 the Gartner Group estimated that by 2003 the average knowledge worker would waste 30 to 40 per cent of their time looking for lost papers (for 'papers' now 'read emails'). The answer is to attack your inbox using the 'Four Ds' principle:

The 'Four Ds' principle

- **D**eal with it there and then.
- **D**elete – read it, decide if you need to keep it and if not delete it.
- **D**elegate – if someone else can handle the matter, pass it to them.
- **D**efer – you may need time to consider your response. Highlight the email in some way and add a reminder for when it needs bringing forward.

The objective of the 'Four Ds' is to leave as few old emails as possible in your inbox. Your inbox should be your work-in-progress file. To be more productive, it must be quick and easy to spot emails which are new or still need your attention. Let's take a look at the 'Ds' in more depth.

Deal with emails now

Many emails can and should be answered immediately. Keep the reply simple and file or delete it once you have replied. When the reply is not quite so simple, choosing to action an email rather than defer it can sometimes be difficult and will depend on what other tasks you have in hand. A useful rule of thumb is the 'Swiss Cheese' approach developed originally by the time management guru Alan Lakein and then coined as the 'two-minute' rule by David Allen in his book *Getting Things Done*.

The two-minute rule

Set yourself a time limit, such as two minutes, for dealing with any one email, rather than assigning it the defer status. Sometimes you may be able to deal with the whole email. At other times it might just be about working out what else is needed, who you need additional input from, and sending out emails to those people.

Priorities will play a part, but the key is not to get so involved that you suddenly find that you have spent all your time dealing with one email when there were other more urgent ones. Perhaps the response required is so complex that nothing else is getting done and there is still a pile of new emails which could have been quickly cleared based on the two-minute principle. The trick is to identify quickly which emails will require considerable time at the expense of other less important ones and allocate specific time to that task.

If you expect a response from an email within a certain time-frame, highlight it or place it in a separate folder: for example, one called 'Awaiting Responses'. You can do this for either the original or your response. Whatever happens, don't leave it unmarked, relying on your memory. You will forget and that might cost a sale, a missed client action or worse.

Delete the trivial emails and multiple copies of email chains

You might be surprised to know that men are far better at deleting emails than women, who tend to be hoarders. We are all guilty of keeping far too many trivial emails: *meet you at 1.00 pm*, *thanks*, newsletters, reminder about today's training, etc. In *Take Back Your Life!* Sally McGhee suggests you need only keep 20 to 30 per cent of the emails you receive each day. My research indicates it might be nearer 50 per cent.

That is still a lot of email. Most of us keep emails 'just in case', 'to cover our backsides' and to be able to say 'but I told you so'. The truth is, such behaviour leads to a poor working culture and relations. It's far better to talk than re-send an email when someone has defaulted on an action.

The only emails you should keep are those which are potentially contractually binding: for example, a change of resources needed to complete a task, a note from a supplier about a date for returning goods, records of discounts, agreement to go ahead. If in doubt about whether or not to keep an email ask yourself these questions:

- Do I need to keep this email for compliance, because it contains information which is legally binding (evidence in an HR tribunal, breach of contract, etc.)?
- If it's a newsletter or similar, is this the only source?
- Will I need this information again in a month's time?

If the answer to these questions is no, delete the email after reading it. If it's yes, then keep it somewhere safe.

Some of you will have specialist archiving software which will effectively scan your inbox and save all these emails to an external secure source such as Mimecast, Enterprise Vault and Autonomy ZANTAZ. In this case you need keep even fewer as they can all easily be restored from the archive vault.

Delegate

Cast your mind back to the premise discussed in the Introduction that your inbox is a DNA fingerprint of you. This is never more true than dealing with incoming email traffic. For example, if you like to ponder or, worse, are a perfectionist, then I'll bet your inbox has lots of emails which still need action and could have been dealt with by someone else. But there they sit while you dither, fearful that no one else will answer them as well as you. Forget it. Delegate, delegate and delegate.

delegate, delegate and delegate

brilliant tip

When you open an email, ask yourself, 'Am I the best person to deal with this or is there someone else who either could or should action it?'

Forward all emails that could and should be handled by others in whatever direction is appropriate – sideways, down and even up. When forwarding down, if needs be, use it as a training opportunity. You could get the delegated person to draft a reply for you to check before it's sent.

Do you need to stay in the loop?

A sure way to drive up the volume of email traffic is keeping yourself in the loop once you have delegated.

brilliant example

The operations director of a quarry producer was promoted to managing director for his unit. In his old job he was responsible for ordering special tags to label the bags of minerals. When he received an email request for this task in his new position he passed it to the new operations director. Still people emailed him. This went on for a few months and started to annoy him. I asked if he had told everyone about his and their new responsibilities and made it clear that he did not need to be involved in the ordering process. A short email to everyone, followed by a note when forwarding any stray ordering emails, quickly decreased this aspect of his email traffic. When he forwarded the emails he simply reminded people that he did not need to be kept in the loop.

To reduce email traffic and save time, be clear about whether or not you need to remain involved. If not, say so when forwarding the email to the appropriate person.

Deferring action – and keeping track of the email

When you decide to defer action by more than a day, first and foremost let the recipient know. Secondly, manage their expectations and try to avoid the need for them to reply. Simply say something like: 'Thanks for your email. I will reply on Friday by noon unless you tell me this is not OK. Only reply if it is not OK.'

brilliant dos and don'ts

Do

● Develop a process of keeping track of emails that still need to be actioned. Here are the five most commonly used ways:

1 Mark it as unread.

2 Flag it – preferably with a reminder.

3 Move it to a pending folder.

4 Print it.

5 Convert it to either a task or calendar reminder.

Don't

● Ask recipients if deferring is OK as this will lead to another round of emails. It also leaves the door wide open for them to say no and hence manage you.

In Outlook, converting email to either a task or calendar reminder is easily achieved by dragging and dropping it to the calendar/task pad. In other email software such as Notes, Entourage and Thunderbird there is usually an option under the 'Tools' menu to create automatically a calendar/task entry.

Which method you choose is a matter of personal preference. My PA uses the fifth option to create a calendar/task entry and it's very effective for her. My personal preference is to mark emails as unread and sometimes use reminder flags.

The brilliant timesaver is to find a way which works for you that ensures you meet deadlines and follow up on outstanding actions. This chosen process should also be used to keep track of emails you send and which need timely replies.

Using your email software to help you – preview panes and other functions

One question that often arises in workshops is whether or not to use the preview/reading pane to help you deal with your inbox. This is largely a matter of personal preference. Many find that the preview/reading lures them into scanning rather than actually handling each email properly. On the other hand, the preview/reading pane can help you spot important items more quickly.

In Outlook, if you open each email fully, there are a range of buttons and icons that can help you handle each email and then view the next one, without having constantly to scroll up and down and move in and out of the inbox (Figure 1.2).

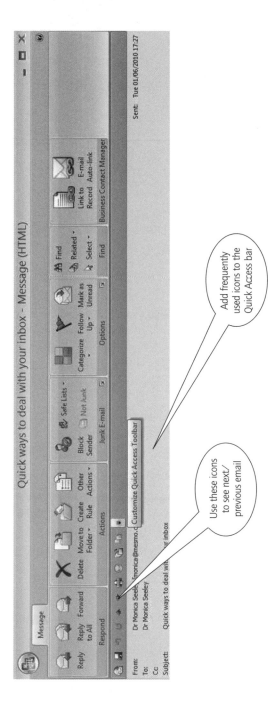

Figure 1.2 Outlook timesaving icons

brilliant recap

- Prioritise your day according to the tasks you need to complete.

- Don't let your day be dominated by email.

- In a normal day, unless you are in a front-line support role, limit checking your emails to a maximum of five times a day.

- As part of the PA/manager relationship, make sure you discuss and review expectations about how often email is checked and its priority in relation to other aspects of your role.

- Adopt the 'Four Ds' principle: handle each email only once. Deal, Delete, Delegate or Defer action.

- When delegating, be clear as to whether or not you need to be kept in the loop.

- Set a limit to how long you spend dealing with each email so that a single message does not engulf your time at the expense of other important messages.

- Develop a foolproof process to ensure that you do not lose sight of the emails you still need to action.

- Set realistic and achievable email response times, and educate others to adopt them.

- Use your out-of-office message to manage people's expectations – especially those in front-line support roles.

CHAPTER 2

Dealing with the email backlog after being away

I figure this is my time – to relax, be with my family, and have a normal life.

Sidney J. Harris

This chapter will help you avoid being deluged with email when you are away from the office or on leave. In particular, you will learn some smart, timesaving ways to view your inbox.

Should I switch off or keep checking email when I go on leave?

This question comes up time and again from people, whether or not they have an assistant. A survey I conducted showed that 50 per cent of executives logged on while on leave (see www. brilliant-email.com). Not because their business expected them to, but because they felt they must. Is this addiction or fear of missing out? Chapter 6 deals with email addiction.

Email is one of the great stress-creators of modern 21st-century office life. Perceived wisdom used to be 'leave email at home when you go on holiday', but with the advent of our 24/7 society and the merging of work and leisure this is changing. Professor

email is one of the great stress-creators

Cary Cooper, the stress management guru, says, 'Logging in on holiday destroys the main purpose of taking a break, namely to rest, relax and unwind.' His advice, which I endorse, is 'If you absolutely must check your email while on leave then only do it once at the end of the day. Don't ruin your family or friends' day by logging on during the morning. If you can resist then wait until the last day of your break.'

Smart ways to view the inbox – especially after being out of the office

One of the frequent questions I am asked is, 'When I have been out of the office for a week or even a day or two, what is the best way to sort the pile of emails in the inbox?' The first and most important step is to make an appointment with yourself to deal with your email. Block out the first hour or two on your return to sort your inbox.

Before you go on leave or out of the office for a day, make sure you have used 'Rules' (see below) to automatically move news-letters and non-important emails to folders.

brilliant timesaver

To set up a 'Rule' to move emails automatically to a folder, go to 'Tools'/'Rules and Alerts' and click on 'New Rule' and follow the 'Rules Wizard' (Figure 2.1). Pick the type of 'Rule': for example, move messages from someone to a folder and then click on the hyperlinked portions in Step 2 and complete. Then press 'Next' to set any exceptions until you come to the 'Finish rule set-up' page: make sure you have ticked the box marked 'Turn on this rule' and press 'Finish'.

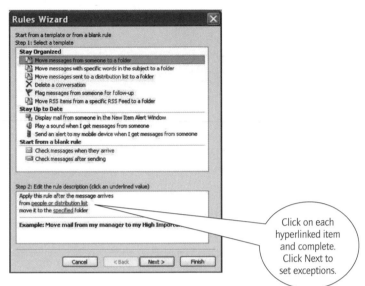

Click on each hyperlinked item and complete. Click Next to set exceptions.

Figure 2.1 Rules Wizard

On your return, to sort and deal with all the emails that have accumulated in your absence, first decide on the best way for you to sort them. For example, look for chains and multiple emails on the same topic and group them together in date order. You then only need to read the most recent missive and delete the rest. Below are some more timesaving ways to quickly sift your inbox and keep to the 'Four Ds' principle of handling each email only once.

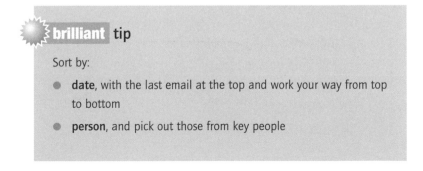

brilliant tip

Sort by:

● **date**, with the last email at the top and work your way from top to bottom

● **person**, and pick out those from key people

- **subject**, and read the last email in a thread first as it probably contains a good number of those listed afterwards
- **emails only 'To' you.**

In Outlook you can sort with two columns. Sort first by the main column (such as 'Date'), then hold down the shift key and click on the second column. Alternatively use the 'Show in Groups' view – see Figure 2.2.

Previews and reading panes

As discussed in Chapter 1, the major drawbacks of these previews and reading panes is that they lure you into cherry picking. Nonetheless, if you have used 'Rules' to sort emails into folders, the preview/reading pane can be most useful when you are looking through a folder of lower-order priority emails (newsletters, out-of-office messages, etc.).

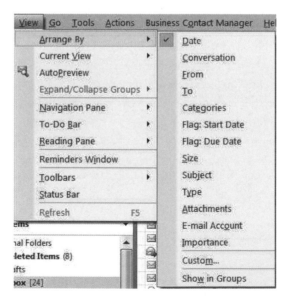

Figure 2.2 Viewing emails in groups

Changing your view

Another easy way to sort your inbox is to change how it looks to suit you. For example:

- Add other columns – for example, 'Cc' to show who else is copied in.
- Filter the inbox – for example, to show only emails where you are in the 'To' line.
- Categorise emails – for example, by project, person, topic. *Possible*
- Make fields editable *in situ*. If someone keeps sending emails with the same subject line you can enable the subject field to be editable and change the subject to something more meaningful for you. *?*

Not all software and versions offer the same level of sophistication.

In Outlook, to view emails by new fields/columns (for example, 'Cc') right-click on any existing field and pick 'Field Chooser' (Figure 2.3). Pick the required field (for example, 'Cc') and drag and drop it beside an existing field. Then you can sort on the new one.

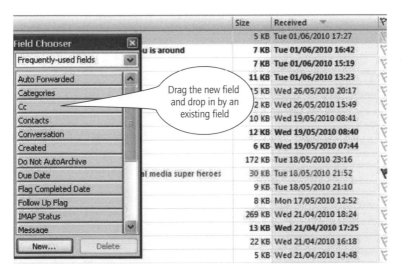

Figure 2.3 'Field Chooser'

To customise other aspects of how you view your mailbox, go to 'View/Current View/Customize View' and then select the required field. For example, to make fields editable *in situ*, select 'Other Settings' and tick the box marked 'Allow in-cell editing' (Figure 2.4).

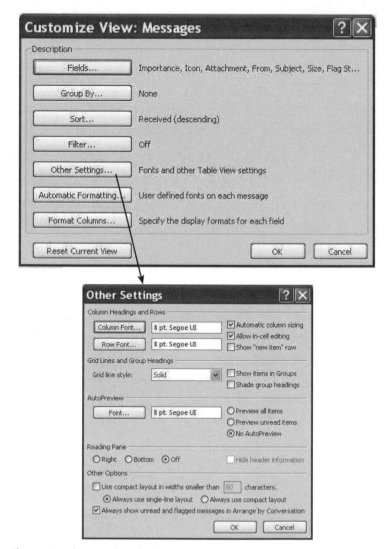

Figure 2.4 'Customize View'

brilliant recap

- Use the functionality of your email software to change how you view your inbox (and associated folders). This will make it easy for you to process your emails, especially if you have a backlog after an absence.

- Take time out from dealing with your email, especially when you are on leave. Remember that it is OK to switch off your BlackBerry, iPhone and other such devices.

- If you must check your email while on leave, then only do it once at the end of each day or on the day before you return to the office.

CHAPTER 3

Prioritise to reduce unnecessary emails

Develop an uncanny ability to be selectively ignorant.

Timothy Ferriss

Email traffic has grown exponentially. Today, it's not uncommon to receive over 100 emails a day. For PAs who look after multiple mailboxes, the volume handled can easily rise significantly. Here we focus on prioritising – specifically:

- Distinguishing between the emails you really need (information) and the nice-to-have-but-perhaps-unnecessary emails (noise).
- Processes to prioritise what information and emails you really need.
- Alternative communication sources for low priority information.
- Ways to say 'no, thank you' to unnecessary emails.

How much of all this email do we really need?

Roughly 80 per cent of the information we need comes from 20 per cent of what we receive. Which is the vital 20 per cent for you? For most of us the real cause of email stress is not the volume of emails but the information overload caused by trying to absorb so much data – much of which is irrelevant.

Your email overload index and its cost

Fill out the following table:

Table 3.1 Email overload index

1 How many emails do you receive on a typical day?	
2 How many of those do you really need?	
3 Subtract your answer to row 2 from your answer to row 1.	
4 Divide the result of your answer to row 3 by the initial total in row 1.	
5 Convert to a percentage (multiply the number in row 4 by 100).	

Row 5 gives you the percentage of emails that you do not need. These are clogging up both your mailbox and your brain. Now plot the value from row 5 on the scale in Figure 3.1 to benchmark your level of information overload.

Less than 15%	15 – 25%	25 – 50%	50 – 75%	Over 75%
No overload	A little overloaded	Overloaded	Quite overloaded	Excessively overloaded

Figure 3.1 Volume of unnecessary email

To calculate the cost of this information overload, either go to www.brilliant-email.com and use the cost of email misuse calculator, or use the template in Table 3.2.

Table 3.2 Email misuse calculator

1 Take the value from row 3 in Table 3.1.	
2 Multiply the value in row 1 above by 1.5 to see the minutes you waste per day.	
3 Divide the value from row 2 by 60 to convert to hours.	
4 Multiply the value in row 3 by your hourly salary.	

This is the minimum amount of time and money you are wasting each day.

The cost of email overload stress

Stress makes heavy inroads into personal and business productivity. A 2009 survey of British civil servants found long hours increased the risk of a heart attack by 60 per cent. In 2008 the Health and Safety Executive estimated that stress-based sick leave costs the UK about £3.7 billion per year. To treat and reduce the level of email overload, we need to address the issue of information overload.

> address the issue of information overload

To a large extent the treatment lies in your own hands. You can control how much email you receive by prioritising your information needs and applying the 80:20 rule.

Simply deleting unnecessary emails on sight is not the answer, because each time you have to make a judgement about what you do not need. Continually deleting unnecessary emails wastes time and lowers your personal productivity (as you will have discovered if you did the exercise in Table 3.1). Finally, for those concerned about their carbon footprint, it's wasting valuable server space, processing power and energy.

Noise versus information in your mailbox

For everything you have missed, you have gained something else, and for everything you gain, you lose something else.

Ralph Waldo Emerson

In the case of email, what you gain and what you lose is time. Have you ever missed a critical piece of information in your inbox which could have resulted in disaster? For the majority of us (including myself) the answer is a resounding 'No'. If the information is that important we hear about it somehow – usually word of mouth, an emailed link from a client or friend, the radio, TV, social networking and so on.

We are overwhelmed with communication channels bringing us news and information. However, we are often reluctant to slim down what floats unbidden into our mailbox for fear of missing that vital email.

 **brilliant** definitions

Your mailbox contains two basic types of emails:

Noise

Emails that add no real value to how you do your job or live your life.

Information

Emails that you need to accomplish your job and live your life (whether you are the CEO of a multinational or a freelance journalist).

So what do you really *really* want?

This section focuses on how to:

● Reduce if not eliminate noise.

● Handle information more effectively.

(Spam from external sources is dealt with separately in Chapter 18.)

Only you know what you need and what is really useful to you. So stop complaining about how much email you receive and take action now. You can prevent low priority emails ever reaching your mailbox and divert all the medium priority ones away from the main inbox.

Several good time management books contain in-depth process-based methodologies for prioritising what you need. Among my favourites are David Allen's *Getting Things Done* and Sally McGhee's *Take Back Your Life!*. Drawing on some of their ideas and my work with clients, here is a quick and easy way to audit your inbox. It's called QSPER and will rapidly reduce the volume of emails you receive. (QSPER was first published in *Managing in the Email Office* by Seeley and Hargreaves.)

Auditing your information needs – the QSPER framework

QSPER in action

Here is how to apply the process and some self-assessment exercises to help you. Create a folder (called 'Audit') with two sub-folders called 'Action' and 'Information'. Review each email

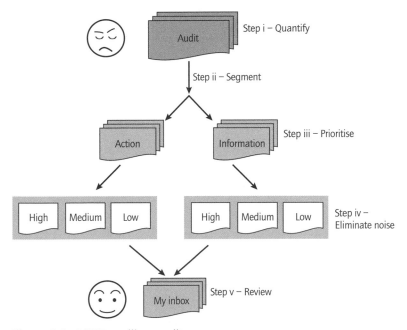

Figure 3.2 QSPER mailbox audit process

and move it to either the Action or Information folder. A quick way is to sort by subject or sender. Go through each email in each sub-folder and assign it a priority of importance of high, medium or low. (For more information on QSPER see www. brilliant-email.com.)

Action emails – self-assessment exercise

Use the template of questions in Table 3.3 to help you prioritise the 20 percent of emails you really need in your inbox. It can be difficult to be tough on yourself and often it helps to have an outside person work with you on the audit.

Table 3.3 Email audit

Question	Priority (for you)	Action
It's urgent/important and only I can deal with it.	H	Deal with these promptly.
I need to deal with it but it can wait.	M	Mark for attention later using one of the methods discussed in Chapter 1 (flag, mark as unread, park in a folder, etc.)
Why am I being asked to deal with this matter when it does not relate to my role?	L	Ask the sender why they asked you in the first place and move it out of your inbox into a pending folder until you are sure about dealing with it. Then decide the priority.

This audit process will help identify and reduce lower priority 'action' emails. Many people hang on to emails which should be delegated to others for action. These emails sit unattended in their inboxes until either a reminder arrives or the lack of action blows them up into a crisis. Delegation reduces the volume of unnecessary action emails and is a powerful tool to coach others. It will save you and the sender time in the long term, and enable you both to be more productive.

Your exit strategy

Surround yourself with the best people you can find, delegate authority and don't interfere.

Ronald Reagan

For examples of text to use when delegating, to make it clear about your continued level of involvement, go to www.brilliant-email.com.

brilliant tip

When delegating emails, ask yourself if you need to be kept in the loop. Make it clear when forwarding the email how you want to be kept informed of progress.

Push back unwanted email

The best bosses will be those who learn to swim amid all the information swirling around them.

Carol Barts

To some extent, emails containing noise, low-value or 'nice-to-see' information are easier to prioritise. To help rank their importance to you, try the following questions:

- Do I need this information to do my job?
- What would happen if I ignored this information?
- This information is 'nice to have' but would I want it if I had to pay for it?
- Can I find this information easily on my own, i.e. use a search engine?
- Can I get the information from several newsletters from one source – for example, a RSS feed?

Regularly review the newsletters you receive because:

● your interests will change

● their quality changes and hence their usefulness

● the frequency of sending changes. Often a weekly round-up is as good as a daily bulletin.

Over the last year I have reduced by about 50 per cent the number of individual newsletters which plop into my inbox by turning to social networking, especially Twitter, to follow people, sites or groups relevant to my interests.

What if you can't unsubscribe?

Your right to receive and, conversely, have your name removed from an external mailing is governed by the Data Protection Act and regulated by the Information Commissioner. Under the Privacy and Electronic Communications Regulations 2003 there is a legal obligation that unsolicited email marketing (unless to an existing customer) is prohibited and that, even if consent is given, an unsubscribe option must be offered on each occasion. Many organisations either do not realise this or try to flaunt these regulations.

Common scenarios are:

● You have asked politely to be removed and nothing happens after three attempts.

● There is no obvious way to unsubscribe.

The Direct Marketing Association's website (www.DMA.org.uk) provides excellent advice on one's rights both as a sender and recipient of email marketing. If the sender of unwanted emails will not remove you from their mailing list, you should report them to the DMA and/or the Information Commissioner's Office (www.ico.gov.uk). My own and others' experiences is that an email warning the sender of your intentions to do this results in speedy action.

Cc'd email

On workshops and in one-to-one coaching sessions, Cc'd email is always given as the number one source of email overload and stress. The perpetual question is 'How can I reduce the amount of emails Cc'd to me and circulating in my business?' The simplest way is to ask people to remove you from their distribution lists. See www.brilliant-email.com for templates of text you can use in this situation.

> ask people to remove you from their distribution lists

Other tactics for dealing with unwanted Cc'd email include:

● Creating a 'Rule' to send all emails with your name in the Cc box to a separate folder.

● Using filters so you only see emails where you are in the 'To' box.

Often though, you need to look a little deeper at the issue of Cc'd email. Email is frequently the wallpaper covering much deeper cracks in the organisation, faulty lines of communications, mistrust, misunderstandings, and, of course, good old 'cover my backside' office politics. See Chapter 11 for more on using the right address box.

he USMT → Dear all
    + Dear X....
    + Please advise..✓

In times of crisis

In times of uncertainty, the volume of email noise often rises as people feel the need to communicate (by email) to try to gain some insight and clarity about the situation. This was demonstrated by an analysis of the email traffic during Enron's demise (see Jim Giles's 'Email patterns can predict impending doom' in the *New Scientist*, 22 June 2009). To avoid becoming caught up in this, ways to reduce the volume of unnecessary email include:

● Setting up a dedicated page on the intranet.

● Using social media tools such as a Facebook page, chatrooms and/or instant messaging.

brilliant example

On reviewing his Cc'd emails, an IT director realised that, although he had told his team he did not need to be copied in, they were still putting him in the Cc box. His solution? During one-to-one meetings he told each person what he did and did not want to see and talked through how they felt about this. He says 'I now use email differently. In principle I only read emails directly addressed to me. This means I get much less Cc'd mail as my team know how I like to operate. If they Cc me I know it's a hidden message saying they want me to get involved.'

For more information on this example see www.brilliant-email.com.

In some situations, there is a need to take a serious look at the team or organisational culture and how email is used. Consider the chart in Figure 3.3 taken from the analysis of one director's inbox which was managed by his PA.

Fifty per cent of emails sent to the director never ever reached him. This data was shown to his team who were astounded to realise how little he actually read of what they sent to him. Some

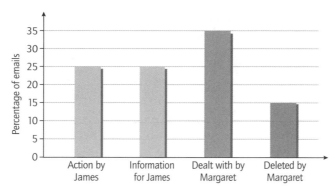

Figure 3.3 Typical waste in an executive's inbox

email best practice and useful tips and hints were provided. This exercise quickly helped people realise the amount of unproductive time spent dealing with unnecessary emails and helped them to focus on what is important to them. The team reduced the emails they sent to him, especially the Cc'd emails.

 example

One executive was so fed up with all the emails about cakes for tea cluttering up her inbox that she set up a rule to send all such messages to the delete folder. Not only did she save herself some time dealing with her inbox – but she said she also lost weight!

I manage someone else's mailbox, what can I do?

If you are a PA or executive assistant managing another person's inbox and you find yourself deleting many of their emails, audit their inbox (as outlined above) to demonstrate to that person just how much of your own time you are wasting. It is usually a good wake-up call, as illustrated in Figure 3.3.

It really is worth spending a little time doing a more in-depth audit and using the results to educate those you work with. It will reduce the level of unnecessary email you receive and reduce their email overload as well.

Try to identify guidelines on:

- what to send to you and what to send to other people (for example, the manager)
- when the manager needs to be Cc'd (for example, for events or emails from key people)
- at what point in a decision/negotiation/sales cycle, the manager should be involved.

Can multiple email addresses help?

In business, many people receive emails directed to them by their name and also by their function (Head of Mathematics Department, Head of Customer Services, Editor, etc.). Multiple email addresses can help in this situation. The main downside is having two mailboxes to check. However, if you use the tools and techniques outlined above, you will be able to prioritise ruthlessly how new email is handled.

At home, it pays to guard your primary email address (both in business and in your social life) and have a second one for general use, for signing up for special offers, vendors at conferences, etc. I use my Hotmail address for all non-business emails, newsfeeds of peripheral and passing interest, and when I suspect that the organisation may not be as judicious as they should about the Data Protection Act.

guard your primary email address

Three active email accounts is probably the maximum most of us can handle. If you have more, consider merging some accounts and consolidating all the email. The sender can still use the email address you gave them, but you view all emails in one place.

wimbledon_SW19 @ yahoo.co.uk.
robertbr_1010 @ yahoo.com

Construct
another ?

Sent-to-received ratio

One final way to reduce the number of emails you need to handle each day is to consider the number of emails you send. The volume of emails sent is often directly correlated to the number received. Carry out the exercise in Table 3.4 to see how you could reduce the number of emails you send – and the number you receive.

Working out your sent-to-received ratio

Count how many emails you send today. Audit your incoming emails and calculate your sent-to-received ratio. Ideally it should be around one sent to three received.

Table 3.4 Your sent-to-received ratio

	Type	Number
1	Received	
2	Sent	
3	Sent-to-received ratio (1:2)	

If your sent-to-received ratio is nearer one sent to five received, review your sent items. See if there is scope to reduce the amount of email you send. If it's much higher, say one sent to ten received, then you probably have far too many newsletters and the QSPER exercise (page 37) should help you redress the balance.

To reduce the number of emails you send, ask yourself:

- How many times did you email the same person?
- Did each email you sent add value for the recipient?
- Could the content of the email have waited until you saw that person?
- Are you forwarding too many emails without much thought as to what you expect the recipient to do?

 **brilliant** recap

It's your inbox and what enters it is totally under your control. If you have too much noise in your inbox you are the only one who can prioritise and reduce the volume of email you need to handle. Senders are not mind readers. So:

● Be ruthless in auditing your inbox.

● Check that the ratio of sent-to-received is under 1:5.

● Tell senders when you don't want their emails, whether politely or assertively.

● Unsubscribe from all low interest external newsletters.

● Invoke the folder by 'Rule' principle for all emails you consider of medium to low priority and for those you cannot remove yourself off the circulation list.

● Discuss with your team who needs what emails and draw up some team guidelines.

● Review your information needs and priorities every six months.

CHAPTER 4

Save time
filing and
finding emails

There is a huge stress with disorganisation and there is also a cost to being disorganised.

Carolee Cannata

HCh 2003 - 2008

The way you folder (or don't folder) emails is part of your email DNA fingerprint, as highlighted in the Introduction. In seven out of ten cases, I find that there is a direct correlation between the state of a person's desk or workspace and their inbox. This chapter covers:

- the pros and cons of using folders to park your emails
- what makes an effective folder structure
- guidelines and templates for implementing your own folder structure
- tips on how to start and keep on track.

To folder or not to folder ...

There are those who meticulously file each email and have a complex hierarchical folder structure with a large number of main folders and sub-folders (often in the hundreds). They will park each email in a folder after reading it, regardless of which of the 'Four D's' category it falls into – Deal, Delete, Delegate or Defer (see Chapter 1). Their aim is a clear empty inbox – what author and broadcaster Merlin Mann terms Inbox Zero – until the next avalanche of new email arrives (see http://inboxzero. com). Others just leave them all in their inbox.

Neither approach is right nor wrong. The key is not to let email pile up unread in your inbox. One of the major email time thieves is scrolling up and down looking for things. All email software has some level of search function (from fairly basic to quite granular and sophisticated). However, these still often return several screens of potentially relevant emails through which you then have to scroll.

If you feel you could never be organised enough to folder your emails and can't function unless you are surrounded by piles of disorganised papers and email, then skip this chapter. If you want to improve your personal productivity then read on.

The pros and cons of folders

A good filing system is critical for processing and organizing your stuff.
David Allen

Benefits of using folders

- Searching is faster, especially if you use a preview or reading pane.
- Housekeeping (for example, deleting old emails) takes less effort.
- You can use 'Rules' (see page 24) to move less important emails out of the main inbox, enabling you to see important emails more easily.
- You can create 'confidential' folders into which certain emails can be moved automatically during times when someone else is dealing with your email (for example, when you're on leave.)

- Significant increase in the feeling of being in control of your mailbox because there are fewer emails in the main inbox.

- Makes it easier to keep within your mailbox limits. Being shut out of your inbox because you are over the limit is perhaps one of office life's most stressful moments, especially when you need to send something urgently.

Downsides of using folders

- It takes time to set up and maintain a good folder structure. (Merlin Mann suggests that foldering is a total waste of your time, given the power of today's search engines.)   ✓ Yes .

- All inboxes and their folders need housekeeping – clearing out those emails past their sell by date and those which if kept might constitute a breach of compliance with the Data Protection Act.

- Folders are not suited to everyone's personality or behaviour and can cause some people more stress and anxiety than leaving all their emails in the inbox.

- Despite the fact that mobile devices like the iPhone, BlackBerry and Android smartphones are now so sophisticated, synchronising folders and seeing emails stored in folders can still be sufficiently problematic as to deter even the most organised person.

The verdict

Overall, most time management experts, organisation gurus and psychologists would promote using a sound reliable folder structure as the foundation for increased productivity and less stress.

Additionally, I think there are probably many lost business

opportunities in large inboxes. In early 2000, the Delphi Consultancy Group estimated that every piece of paper in a business costs US $120 and, despite that, around 15 per cent of them are lost. That's quite an overhead for any business even before you consider the potential lost business opportunities among the lost paper. For 'paper', these days read 'email'. Many who do not believe in foldering have huge inboxes containing thousands of emails and most have no idea what is in their inbox beyond the first two viewing screens.

What makes an effective folder structure?

– 3U Secs –

It should take you less than one minute to pick something up out of your in-basket or print it from an email.

David Allen

View your email folders as you would a filing cabinet. Decide on the top-level structure, then add some sub-folders and sub-sub-folders if necessary. For example:

- Projects
- Pending
- Current – to action
- Next month – to action
- Clients
- Leads to follow up
- People's names
- Topic (such as 'HR', 'PR')
- Meetings
- Newsletters
- Social matters
- Financial.

Your folders must work for you. Look at the examples on www.
brilliant-email.com and then cherry pick the parts which best
suit you and your business. It's worth giving your folder structure some thought before implementing it, although it's not hard
to add, merge and delete unnecessary ones later down the line.

brilliant dos and don'ts

Do

- Keep the folder system simple and consistent with your role and the
  tasks you do.
- Limit the number of top-level folders to 30.
- Tidy them up regularly – see the section on housekeeping (page 58).
- Keep them current – as projects and interests change, either archive the
  emails or at least demote the folder from being top level. For example,
  I have an 'Old clients' folder within my main top-level folder 'Client'. As
  projects close, the folder is demoted to a sub-folder of the 'Old clients'
  sub-folder.

Don't

- Make the folder structure so complex that it takes you too long to
  decide where to file an email.
- Create unnecessary sub-folders; any folder with less than ten emails is
  probably redundant.

Stop hoarding

One of the sea changes that search engines like Google, Yahoo and
Bing have brought about is the freedom to release yourself from
hoarding all those 'just in case' news emails. If you delete a newsletter, I guarantee you can find the same information on Google
within a couple of minutes. Why weigh down your inbox and slow
down your own search capacity? Alternatively, if you really can't
delete an email, create a 'Pending' folder (shown in Figure 4.1)
and put it there.

 **tip**

The trick with a 'Pending' folder is to make sure you check it
regularly. Set yourself a time limit and, if it becomes clear that
you are not going to action an item, either delete it (usually those
relating to an event), or move it to the 'Miscellaneous' folder.
Before deleting, make sure you have added the sender's contact
details to your address book (contacts list), should you ever want to
reconnect with them.

Sometimes I receive a blizzard of emails relating to a specific
project but, if I'm working on something else at the time, I don't
want to be distracted. Rather than leave them floating in the
main inbox, I add an 'Action Pending' sub-folder (Figure 4.1) to
the main project/client folder so that this influx of new emails can
be parked there until it's time for me to deal with that project.

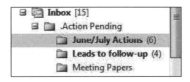

Figure 4.1 My 'Action Pending' folder structure

The folder structure you need will obviously depend on your
role. Here are a couple of examples that impressed me.

 **example**

James Lapage, Managing Director at Hoburne Holiday Parks

I have a folder for each of my divisional heads who report directly to me.
The folders start with a full stop so that they appear at the top of my folder
list. In each I have a sub-folder that is headed 'Current' and also sub-folders

for major projects or tasks they are working on. When that project or task is finished I move the sub-folder into a permanent folder. I also have a folder for departments such as 'Accounts' and 'Computer', as well as one for 'Reports' and 'Items to read later'.

When James prepares for his one-to-one with each manager, a review of their email folder quickly gives him a list of topics he needs to discuss. Again, no frittering away valuable time searching for emails.

 **example**

Donna Washtall, PA

I create a 'Meetings' folder that contains folders within it for each month of the year. (You can get them to order themselves chronologically by numbering them 01 January, 02 February and so on.)

Any emails relating to meetings (confirmations/agendas/maps, etc.) can be dropped into the appropriate month as they arrive and then brought forward when needed. This saves me cluttering up my inbox or a 'Pending' folder and also saves a lot of searching time.

Figure 4.2 Donna's impressive 'Meetings' folder structure

To have a frequently used folder appear at the top of the list, start the name with either a full stop or a space (for example, '.Pending'). Alternatively, if your software allows, place it in the 'Favourite' space as shown in Figure 4.3.

One email, two folders

'Ah, but,' the doubters say. 'One email often relates to at least two different topics (such as "Project" and "Person")'. The answer to that is that most email software systems allow you to copy an email. For example, users of:

● Outlook – use the 'Copy to Folder' option on the 'Edit' menu.

● Entourage – use the duplicate function 'Edit/Duplicate' and then move the duplicate to the other folder.

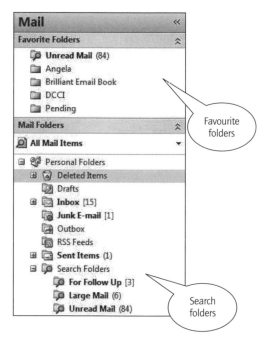

Figure 4.3 'Favourites' and 'Search' folders

Exploit the features of your software

Most software contains useful functions for organising and searching your folders.

Searching and keeping the searches for future use

How often do you search your entire mailbox (i.e. inbox and all the folders) for emails from a particular person, on a specific topic of a particular type, and then need to re-do the search again for whatever reason? Whatever the reason, this is another of those frustrating timewasting tasks. It doesn't have to be that way.

Many email software packages provide a facility to create a 'Search folder'. These are like virtual views across your mailbox folders and they are automatically updated as relevant emails arrive (for example, 'Unread'). You can keep them for instant re-referral and, even better, they do not take up valuable mailbox space.

- Outlook 2003 and onwards provides a set of pre-defined 'Search folders', as shown in Figure 4.3.
- Entourage also provides a set of extensive pre-defined folders. To create a new one go to 'File/New Saved Search' and search as usual, but this time click on the 'Save' button (top right).

These are great timesavers if you need to keep searching on the same topic or person. For example, I use the 'Unread' one to check for new newsletters, which saves me time checking each folder.

Use 'Rules' to automatically park emails as they arrive

One of the most under-utilised function in all mail software (where it exists) is the 'Rules' function, which enables you to move emails automatically to a folder. It's the equivalent of the 'Get Out of Jail' card in Monopoly.

> move emails automatically to a folder

'Rules' have three main benefits:

- They save time manually moving emails to folders.

- They automatically de-clutter the inbox of less important emails, such as newsletters.

- They allow you review many emails on the same topic in one go, which can be a great way of grouping them automatically.

 brilliant timesaver

Use 'Rules' to automatically park new emails as they arrive, without you needing to do anything.

Typical examples of ways people use 'Rules' to handle their inbox more efficiently include:

- Moving all newsletters to a folder(s).

- Out of Office messages – especially after doing a bulk email-shot.

- Meetings/events – many people, especially PAs and executive assistants responsible for arranging meetings, will set up a 'Rule' to move all messages as they arrive to a folder.

- Topics – where there are several threads, and it would be better to read them in one go rather than trying to make a decision piecemeal.

For more on creating 'Rules', see Chapter 2.

Mailbox housekeeping

Regardless of whether or not you use folders, there will come a point at which you have to do some mailbox housekeeping. Most organisations impose some form of limit on the size of

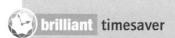 **brilliant** example

In one organisation, the engineers constantly received 'All User' travel updates by email. Not surprisingly, these were useful only if they were travelling. Their solution was to create a 'Rule' to send them all to the 'Deleted' folder, where they could still be checked if needed. Meanwhile, they saved time by not being distracted and having to move these potentially unnecessary emails to a folder.

your personal mailbox. This is true whether your email system is hosted or run in-house.

This is because slim mailboxes are healthy mailboxes. They are easier to restore in the event of a systems outage (the polite way of saying a crash). The larger the mailbox, the more servers you need and the more energy needed to run the servers. Although servers and storage are now relatively cheap, the associated energy costs are still an overhead to the business that can be avoided through proper email housekeeping.

If you use a hosted mail provider, be it free like Hotmail and Yahoo or a specialist service provider like Mimecast, you will find that the cost is proportional to the mailbox size. With free services such as Hotmail there is a space limit beyond which you have to pay.

Good email housekeeping not only reduces the cost of running your email system, but it can also help to increase your personal productivity.

brilliant timesaver

Do your mailbox housekeeping little and often. Aim to keep within 75 per cent of your mailbox limit.

Being over your mailbox's limit is like exceeding the speed limit and seeing an unmarked police car in your rearview mirror. Your heart sinks because you know you will be fined and maybe even suspended for a while.

Here are five tips for maintaining a small and stable inbox. These will make you feel far more in control of your inbox, help reduce your email stress levels and save you time retrieving old emails.

1   Set aside 10 to 15 minutes every few days to tidy up your mailbox.

2   Remove and save large attachments to a folder on the network/hard drive, so they are filed with all the other relevant files. You can find out more about smart ways to manage attachments in Chapters 15 and 16.

3   Delete previous entries in a chain of email; keep only the last one containing all the previous entries.

4   Clean up your sent items folder. Delete attachments – you sent them so you must have them stored elsewhere. Delete your sent email once the person has replied (assuming their reply contains your entry).

5   Folder all sent items at least by year and consider deleting all those which are over five years old. How often have you been asked for an email this old? If you do feel you need to keep a certain email, then leave it, archive it or save it outside the email software as a text file.

Housekeeping software

Most software has functions to allow you to check your mailbox size and help you keep within mailbox limits. For example, in Outlook you can:

● carry out a 'mailbox clean up' (select 'Tools'/'Mailbox Cleanup')

- search folders for large emails.

In Notes you also have a 'Mailbox' quota fuel gauge.

There are also some useful software add-ins which can be purchased and can sort emails automatically, such as Addins-4Outlook (see www.addins4outlook.com) and Neo (see www.caelo.com).

How to get started cleaning up your inbox

> *We said we wouldn't look back.*
>
> Salad Days

If you have not used folders much in the past, the chances are you have several thousand emails sitting there (going back over several years): the thought of sorting through these may be enough to deter you from even starting. Here's a cheeky way to break down that barrier and get you started. You will be able to create a clean inbox and take immediate control of it.

 **timesaver**

Create a new folder called 'Old emails' and move all emails that are over two weeks' old into that folder. Now you should have a relatively clear inbox and be in a position to move forward with your email housekeeping programme.

If you're feeling really energetic, you can then divide this big folder into a few sub-folders by date – for example, one for each year – and file the emails accordingly. When you have a few minutes you can gradually start to delete some of the dead wood by sorting by subject and person and looking for redundant emails and multiple copies of the same discussion. You will be amazed at how good you feel.

Depending on your mailbox size and set-up, you could archive these emails instead of creating a folder in your main mailbox. Just create the 'Old emails' folder as part of your archive. In Outlook these are affectionately called 'pst' files.

Archiving old emails

This is almost the subject of a book in itself. There are basically three ways to archive emails:

- Specialist archiving software such as Mimecast, Enterprise Vault and Autonomy ZANTAZ.
- Outlook 'pst' folders.
- Electronic document management systems, which also store all the associated files for that project (for example, Workspace and Documentum).

Find out what archiving system is available to you and use it to keep within mailbox limits. If you are a business owner, invest in a robust email archiving system either hosted (increasingly the favoured option) or in-house.

For more information on archiving go to www.brilliant-email. com.

brilliant recap

● Regard your inbox as the current work-in-hand folder.

● Do not regard your inbox as a massive unstructured filing system for every email that ever enters your mailbox.

● Create a simple, reliable and robust folder structure where emails can be safely parked.

● Use 'Rules' to park emails automatically as they arrive.

● Keep to within 75 per cent of your mailbox limit.

● Find and use the software tools to help you keep within limits (for example, 'Mailbox cleanup' in Outlook).

● Review your folder structure and the contents every three to six months and clear out any old emails that are no longer needed.

● Invest in dedicated archiving systems as needed.

CHAPTER 5

Give to gain
more time

Planning is an unnatural process; it is much more fun to do something. The nicest thing about not planning is that failure comes as a complete surprise, rather than being preceded by a period of worry and depression.

Sir John Harvey-Jones

This chapter covers how to be more effective by providing enough time for your email recipient. It focuses on how you can:

- improve the use of your time and that of your colleagues by making sure you leave people sufficient time to reply properly to your email
- increase the probability of meeting deadlines, even when others you depend on are unavailable
- further reduce the email stress factor
- promote even better working relationships.

How often have you rushed to complete and email a report only to have an out-of-office message ping back at you? How often do you need an urgent reply from a colleague and have the same thing happen? Both often result in wasted time, missed deadlines and increased levels of stress.

Unrealistic expectations

Email shortens the delivery time but it does not and cannot shorten the thinking time. Rarely does it even shorten the time needed to perform a task such as prepare board papers, revise a sales proposal or rehearse a presentation. Email allows us to leave things to the last minute and expect miracles. You get 'the monkey off your back' and onto someone else's – usually the recipient's.

Downsides of leaving insufficient time for the recipient

Truncated and last-minute delivery times generally only serve to drive up stress levels, wreck working relations and set unrealistic expectations. This is because we have compressed reply times and set impractical and unreasonable deadlines. Other downsides of not planning properly and expecting an immediate reply include:

- Missed deadlines – sometimes with financial repercussions (for example, failing to file a legal action, spot a tender date, miss a news story).
- Poor customer satisfaction – the ultimate recipient (customer, etc.) expects a quick reply. However, internal processes mean that the time it takes to compose a reply can be quite lengthy. This can lead to customer dissatisfaction.
- Incorrect responses – haste increases the risk of producing an inappropriate, sloppy, or even incorrect reply, with possible financial consequences.
- Security breaches – speed increases risk of security and compliance breaches from poorly worded replies.
- Damage to company image and personal reputation – all the above can create an adverse image of the company/individual.

The time you give the recipient is another aspect of your email DNA fingerprint. It creates a perception of you and the

[handwritten marginalia: Pank who pay £12K/year!]

professionalism – or otherwise – of your business in the recipient's mind. It may also suggest that the recipient was bottom of your priority list and not deserving of your full attention and planning.

The benefits of allowing sufficient time for the recipient

The productivity gains to be made from planning ahead and leaving the recipient sufficient time to make a proper reply include:

- Reduced stress levels.
- Better quality replies.
- Customer delight when you reply within the expected timeframe.
- Reduced risk of missing important deadlines.
- Improved professional image of you and your business.
- Better working relationships and an increased 'confidence rating' with the recipient: when you do need an urgent reply they are more likely to accommodate you, seeing it as an exception rather than your usual way of working. *[handwritten: All EHB email to assistant (?)]*

What is a realistic response time?

The crux to providing time for the recipient is having a sensible baseline for what you all feel is an acceptable response time – an 'email service level agreement' just as you would have in many other parts of your business (helpdesk, customer service, etc.).

---

brilliant tip

Half a day or within four hours is the recommended norm for expecting a reply to both internal and external emails.

[handwritten: INTERNAL EMAIL Manages → same day]

Benchmarking exercise

- How quickly do you *expect a reply* to an email you *send*?

- How quickly do you *expect to reply* to emails you *receive*?
- Ask your colleagues how quickly *they think* you want a reply.
- Is there a mismatch between the responses to these questions?
- If there is a mismatch, what do you think is the cause?
- What image do your expectations convey?
- Is this the right image for you (and your business)?

Mind the gap

Figure 5.1 shows the results of a survey conducted for a client. This is what senders say they expect:

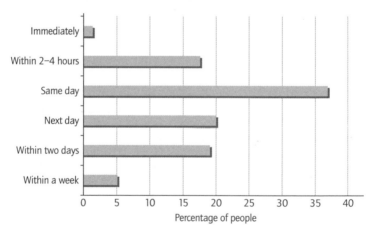

Figure 5.1 Senders' reply expectations

All too often there is a disparity between the perceptions of the sender and recipient about what is expected. Compare this with the results in Figure 5.2 of what recipients in one organisation thought was expected of them.

Forty-four per cent felt that in reality a reply was expected within a couple of hours and nearly a third felt that to reply within a day is acceptable. When the results were presented to

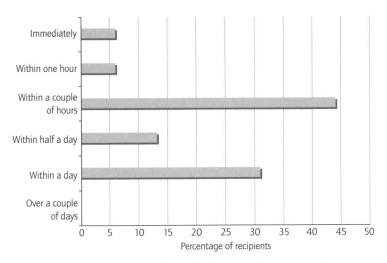

Figure 5.2 Recipients' perception of when a reply is expected

the management team in this organisation, they were visibly shocked at the disparity – they thought everyone understood that half a day was an acceptable response time.

Many managers in other organisations often comment that they are surprised by how quickly people respond to emails that they themselves felt were not that urgent. Equally there are those who *do* expect an instant reply. Journalists are often the worst in terms of expecting an instant reply. Sometimes it's acceptable when in response to a news story. At other times it's just because of bad planning and a deadline creeping up.

PAs often tell me that their manager expects an instant reply. Yet, when challenged about whether they have discussed what is a realistic reply time, few have even discussed this issue.

Like myself, Rob Bamforth, Principal Analyst, Quocirca (the UK research and analysis company) has observed that those with handheld mobile devices often expect a far quicker reply than those operating from a conventional laptop or PC. Part of this lies in, and is driven by, our 'instant gratification' society and the 7/24/365 day culture in which we live. But is it realistic and does it leave sufficient time for a considered reply?

How to establish a realistic response time

To decide what an acceptable response time is for you, consider these three factors:

1 The content of the email – a reasonable response time to a request for guidance on a complex legal issue could easily be a day or two. A revised price structure might be a day.

2 The nature of your business – for example, a request under the Freedom of Information Act must be responded to within 20 days.

3 What is really meant by a 'reply'? – do you mean a full answer or, at the minimum level, an acknowledgement of your email?

Before sending an email, ask yourself, how long will it take me to do this task? Now double it and that is probably a good yardstick of an acceptable response time for your business.

You can refine your baseline reply time, depending on your business, by using the following criteria and sanity checks:

● Review with your colleagues and those you work most closely with what they expect.

● Agree a baseline, and then identify exceptions and how to deal with them (such as by phone).

● Work to these guidelines for a couple of weeks and note the pros and cons.

● Revise as appropriate.

● Incorporate these response times as part of your email best practice policy, contracts, terms and agreements.

● Promote the benefits of working to sensible response times.

- Share these service level agreements (internal and external) on your website, in contracts, in your email signature.

Having a baseline for an acceptable response time often means planning ahead. For example, if you produce the monthly sales report or campaign analysis, then you must make sure that you email those providing the input at least half a day ahead. While that is not always possible, it's fairer than always working to tight deadlines.

You might just be surprised at how well such suggestions are received. It makes working relationships much easier as everyone then knows and is working to the same standards.

> it makes working relationships much easier

Other ways to improve how you work through email

The key is not to prioritize what is on the schedule, but to schedule your priorities.

Stephen Covey

brilliant example

One executive works very early in the morning (around 5.00 am). However, she feels that rarely are the emails she sends so urgent that the recipient needs to respond ahead of their own priorities. To stop the recipients (often her team members) from getting distracted, she delays sending the message.

Leaving time for the respondent allows you to create the right impression. It means that both you and the recipient are operating from a level playing field and you don't impose either your poor planning or sense of urgency on other people. There are a number of other ways you can try to do this:

- Check calendars to see who is available when and then agree a sensible timescale. This is very useful when the person you are working with travels frequently.

- Build in time – when you know your reply has to be reviewed by others, manage the sender's expectation of when they will get a response. For example, in many law practices, replies from juniors and trainees have to be reviewed by a senior partner before being sent externally.

- Establish priorities – and if the matter is urgent and may require some time, discuss current priorities. If there is a mismatch work out how to overcome it. Don't just send an email and expect the person to action the matter.

- Add 'Time Zones' when working with someone in another time zone. To add an extra time zone to your calendar in Outlook, right-click on the left-hand time bar and choose 'Change Time Zone'. Then tick the box 'Show an additional time zone' and choose one from the list (Figure 5.3). Mac and Vista users can add another clock to the desktop.

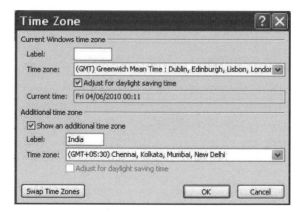

Figure 5.3 Adding an additional time zone

- Manage sender expectations – when you cannot respond within the expected email service level agreement time

CHECK OUT (handwritten)

frame, send a holding email. This manages expectations and says when you will deal with the matter.

- Delay sending your emails. This is very important if you are the boss, because people still deem the boss's emails to be top priority. This can be done in Outlook using the 'Delay Delivery' function. (In a new message, go to 'Options' and click on the 'Delay Delivery'.) Alternatively, leave them in your draft box and send them later in the day.

brilliant tip

When sending holding replies, be clear and firm, saying something like 'I will reply on Friday unless you tell me this is unacceptable'. Don't uses phrases such as 'Is this OK?' It leaves the door open for the sender to say 'No' and put you under pressure. It also encourages another round of unnecessary email exchanges.

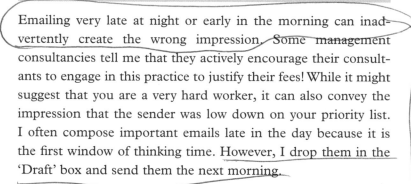

Emailing very late at night or early in the morning can inadvertently create the wrong impression. Some management consultancies tell me that they actively encourage their consultants to engage in this practice to justify their fees! While it might suggest that you are a very hard worker, it can also convey the impression that the sender was low down on your priority list. I often compose important emails late in the day because it is the first window of thinking time. However, I drop them in the 'Draft' box and send them the next morning.

Yes (handwritten)

🔄 **brilliant** recap

- Plan ahead and don't email five minutes before you need a reply.

- As a guideline, allow at least four hours for a reply.

- Share your expectations as a sender and as a recipient; check for mismatches in expectations and how to bridge the gap.

- Broadcast your email service level agreement to all those you work with and include them as guidelines within contracts, terms of engagement, etc.

- Take account of other people's working patterns in order to maximise how and when work is processed, especially if you are the boss.

- If you cannot reply within the terms of the email service level agreement, acknowledge the sender and manage their expectations by informing them when you will reply.

CHAPTER 6

Overcoming email addiction and dependency

Addiction – the state of being enslaved to a habit or practice or to something that is psychologically or physically habit-forming, such as narcotics, to such an extent that its cessation causes severe trauma.

www.thesaurus.com

There is a subtle but important difference between email addiction and email dependency. The former is a personal disposition and behaviour, whereas the latter is about the business culture you work in. This chapter covers:

- email addiction and dependency and the costs to individuals and the business
- how to break the cycle and improve your health
- developing a contingency plan for a serious email systems failure (outage) to ensure business continuity.

 **brilliant** definition

Email addiction

The constant checking of one's email for no particular reason.

Addiction – how widespread it is?

There are those who check their emails every few minutes (even in meetings and on holiday) and do not feel they can live without checking. A survey I conducted in 2007 with Revolution Events for their Inbox–Outbox 2007 event found that over 60 per cent of business users check their email when away from the office. When probed, 20 per cent said it was self-inflicted as they perceived it to be expected of them. For more information see www.brilliant-email.com.

Recently a survey carried out by Osterman Research (an Amerian industry market research company) on behalf of the NeverFail Group, found that in the USA 78 per cent of people even checked email while in the bathroom and 11 per cent said they looked at email during 'intimate moments'. Nearly 80 per cent said they took their mobile devices, which they used to access work email, with them on vacation, and 33 per cent revealed that they hid from family and friends while on vacation just to check email.

Little wonder such devices as the BlackBerry are often called 'CrackBerries'. The damage they can wreak on your *persona* and social life can be as bad as taking hard drugs.

The cost of email addiction

As noted in Chapter 3, work-related stress is costly. Professor Cary Cooper, Professor of Organisational Psychology and Health at University of Lancaster, believes email is a major source of employee anxiety, though quite what proportion is hard to quantify exactly. Nonetheless, there is abundant evidence of email stress.

A study for Veritas in 2005 found that one in five people get angry if they can't immediately access their email. After five minutes a third are 'irate'. After half an hour another third join the irate gang (and feel like kicking the cat!) and after one hour 82 per cent feel irate and stressed. A week of downtime is thought to be more traumatic than divorce and moving house. In the USA some psychiatrists have now suggested that internet addiction should be treated as a psychiatric disorder.

Email addiction therefore has a cost at both a personal and business level. It also means you are often not taking part in what is currently going on around you because your mind is elsewhere.

Creating a healthier work and social lifestyle by reducing email addiction

I am truly stumped by this technology and the people who are doing it [checking their handheld devices] ... You are seated next to Kirk Douglas, Jay Leno, Jane Fonda and Joan Collins and you prefer to hunch over your contraption.

Joan Collins, *Spectator*, 3 April 2010

Are you suffering from email addiction without realising it? Do you want to reduce the risks of email addiction to your health and work–life balance?

brilliant tip

To check your level of email addiction, go to www.brilliant-email. com.

Unlike conventional substance and smoking addictions, there is no medication. Instead, treatment must draw on the ways used to treat alcohol and gambling and adopt a slow withdrawal process.

Here are seven tips to start curing your email addiction and improve your personal wellbeing and relationships, both in and outside work:

1 Switch off all the new email notifications and close/ minimise your email program.

2 Give people an incentive to come and talk to you instead of emailing.

3 Tell people you will no longer have your email always open and ask them to call/talk to you if it's really urgent.

4 Limit the number of times you access your inbox (for example, once every 90 minutes).

5 Fine yourself if you log in between the set times (and make it painful).

6 Celebrate and reward yourself when you reach the target time with no in-between glimpses.

7 If you feel you must check your emails on holiday, then either do it once in the evening or towards the end of the vacation.

If you have a handheld email device (BlackBerry, iPhone, etc.), a dramatic measure would be to lock it away and revert to carrying only a dedicated mobile phone.

In addition, you should reduce the volume of email you need to handle as described in Chapters 1 and 2.

brilliant example

As part of his New Year's resolutions, Tony Johnson, a senior technical manager, decided to reduce both his own and other colleagues' email addiction. He offered an incentive (tea/coffee and biscuits) to people who came to talk to him rather than sent an email. The results: fewer emails and more personal networking, as well as a little lost weight as the edibles he gave away were Christmas gifts.

(handwritten notes) OR pls come + see me @ morning break → staff room / lunch time → main hall + one walk around
> + two walk arounds (4 – 4.30) End of Day

What is email dependency

Email dependency is the perception that everything depends on email and without it no work can be done. Email has come to dominate our lives. Figure 6.1 shows the result of my survey into how often people choose email over other communication methods.

email has come to dominate our lives

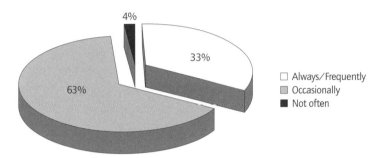

4%

33%

63%

☐ Always/Frequently
▨ Occasionally
■ Not often

Figure 6.1 How often an alternative to email is considered

Only a third always think about using an alternative communications channel to email (e.g. phone/face to face discussion). Yet until about 10 years ago email was a rarity for many. Talking face to face or by telephone, pen and paper, fax or typewritten communication were the mainstays of business communication.

Reducing email dependency

Again there is no medication: the cure lies in helping people realise there are alternatives that are just as effective and sometimes more so. Often it takes a crisis of almost epic proportions as illustrated by the example below.

 **example**

A local authority had a systems outage which lasted for nearly a week. After half a day people started to say they might as well go home as they could not do their work without email. The IT director had to go around and remind people that although they could not send notes and papers by email, they could print them off and either physically take them to their colleagues or use Royal Mail. They could also telephone residents to resolve matters.

Once the systems were re-instated, the IT director decided to implement a set of email best practice guidelines to improve and balance the use of email with other communication methods. They were also designed to reduce the volume of email traffic and size of archive files (which had caused the outage in the first place) and to tackle email dependency throughout the organisation.

The cost of email dependency

In 2005 a report commissioned by CipherTrust (www.cipher-trust.com) estimated that email failures cost UK business £1 billion per year. That's £68,000 a day based on an average company of 200 employees. Quocirca (www.quocirca.com), in their 2008 report, 'Soaring not Surfing', found that, for small-to medium-size businesses, while 25 per cent of businesses said they would lose sales if their system was down for over one hour, the remainder would feel an impact only after a day.

How email dependent is your business?

For how long can you cope without email? What might be the cost to you and your business without it? These are some of the questions you should address using the template in Table 6.1.

Email systems outage

If there was an email systems outage in your business, rate how dependent your business is on email to execute the following tasks/activities. Would you be at risk (and liable for a fine) because you could not process paperwork on time?

Table 6.1 How email dependent is your business?

Task/activity	Email dependency rating – score 1 (low) and 5 (totally dependent)
1 Take/process an order / *new parent full up*	4
2 Exchange information with others (internally and externally), such as planning a project	3
3 Agree contracts	4
4 Arrange meetings	3
5 Process forms, such as timesheets	2
6 Plan/design new product concept	3
7 Close a sale	4
8 Communicate with other members of the team/~~clients~~ *punch.*	5
9 Place a news article	1
10 Manage your team	4
TOTAL	33

Table 6.2 Interpretation and action needed to protect your business

Score	
50 to 30	Identify the highest areas of email dependency and either make changes and/or educate people to think outside the email box. You are probably missing some business opportunities by being so email dependent. Identify the risk to the business of a systems outage and check your contingency plan for such an event.
30 to 10	You have a well balanced business and are probably using email to good advantage. Check your contingency plan and make sure it covers the areas of highest email dependency.

Advise STAFF / MANAGEMENT
→ iPhone / Domino etc.

Email is mission-critical for most businesses. As the local authority example discussed on page 84 demonstrates, we might not be able to function at full capacity but most businesses can still operate. The main cost is usually lost orders, especially if you are an e-business. Customers can and will go elsewhere with their order if they cannot get what they want at the first click. However, some people rejoice when there is no email and see it as an opportunity to get their real day job done rather than drowning in email.

Advantage of Googlemail

Contingency planning for email outages

Access via iPhone tethering

The key is to have a contingency plan for what would happen if your email was down for more than 24 hours. This might include:

- Switching to an alternative delivery mechanism, such as a USB dongle if the actual network is down.
- Switching to an alternative personal email address (for example, Google or Yahoo).
- Outsourcing to a dedicated email hosting supplier organisation like Mimecast. *explore...*
- Switching to cloud computing and using a system like Googlemail.
- Making sure you still have a working fax machine.
- Talking.
- Educating employees to be creative and use other techniques.

brilliant tip

Make sure you have a contingency plan for email outages that encompasses operations at both the personal and business level.

The plan will need to take account of where the fault lies, whether it's the server (the most common cause) or the network (broadband, Ethernet, etc.). For a good review of email contingency planning see Mimecast's white paper 'Email as Part of a Business Continuity Strategy' (www.mimecast.com).

Breaking the email dependency cycle

To help the business reduce its email dependency you need to educate your employees to remain calm and be productive without email. Ways to achieve this include training and occasional email-free periods. It's like testing the fire alarm and evacuating the building in the event of a disaster: you hope it will not happen, but you must be prepared.

> remain calm and be productive without email

Email-free periods

Many companies have email-free periods to reinforce the message that email is not the only way. At Intel on Fridays, for instance, their engineers try to deal with all problems just by talking.

Deloitte ran an email-free campaign for a short while to reinforce the message that sometimes it was more expedient to talk than email. Although they have since dropped the campaign, they say that it achieved the desired effect.

 **brilliant** recap

- Reducing personal email addiction can improve your health and well being.

- If you are suffering from email addiction start by limiting the number of times you access your emails. Let everyone know and ask for their support.

- Leave behind or lock away your mobile email device when on holiday.

- Limit any financial consequences of an email outage by making sure you have a robust contingency plan in place.

- Educate people that email is not the only way and that there is life without email.

- Reviewing and reducing your business email dependency will ensure the business continues to function, and limit the disruption in the event of a systems outage.

- Changing your organisation's level of email dependency may highlight more cost-effective and competitive ways to do business (for example, sometimes a sale can be closed more quickly with a conversation than by email).

PART 2

Communicate more effectively by choosing and using the right channel

'It [electric communications] will never be a substitute for the face of a man, with his soul in it, encouraging another man to be brave and true.'

Charles Dickens

In this part we provide a framework to compare using email to using other communications media. There is advice and templates to help you choose when email is the best channel, when to do things differently and how to minimise the risks when there is no clear choice.

Today, rightly or wrongly, email is the main way that people in business use to communicate. This is why most email best practice guidelines focus primarily on how to reduce the volume of email through prioritising and processing the email traffic through your mailbox. Chapters 1–6 in this book have addressed some of these challenges. The next element to saving time dealing with your mailbox is to decide when to use email and, if you do, how to ensure you convey the right message.

When was the last time you picked up the phone or walked and chatted to a colleague? When I walk into an office it's often eerily quiet. Gone is the buzz generated by people talking and laughing. The only noise is the click-click of the keyboard as everyone has their heads buried in computer screens and, more often than not, their mailboxes.

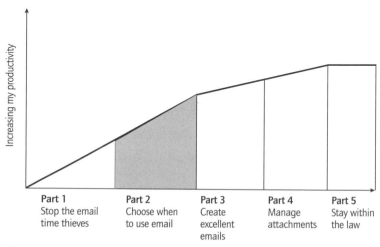

Five steps to improving my productivity – choosing when to use email

Now more than ever before there is a huge array of communications media, from micro-blogs such as Twitter, to instant messaging and conventional face-to-face conversations. It is not always obvious which is the most productive and cost-effective channel. A trade-off and a judgement must be made about what is most important – expediency, confidentiality, the need for an audit trail, etc. Such decisions are often influenced by the state of the business, current priorities and personal location at the time the message must be communicated. The following chapters will help you to get it right.

CHAPTER 7

Email is not the only way

The most important thing in communication is to hear what isn't being said.

Peter Drucker

Email has some inherent strengths and weaknesses, some of which have existed since its invention in the early 1970s. Unfortunately, as is born witness by some of the more prominent email media disasters, email's strengths can also become its weaknesses. This chapter covers:

- a brief history of email and its evolution as a channel of communications
- the importance of remembering that email is only one of many choices of communications media available to you
- how to work out which communications channel to use and when.

In order to capitalise on email's strengths and mitigate its inherent weaknesses, it helps to compare the merits of its use against those of other communications channels such as talking. The well tried and trusted 'media richness' model (see page 98) provides a simple and useful basis for making this evaluation. It gives you a sound foundation on which better decisions can be made about how to use email to maximum advantage.

Take the example of 'Ketchupgate', where a PA in a prominent law firm spilt ketchup on a senior partner's white linen suit. He emailed asking her for the £4 cleaning cost. She was absent at the time he sent it as her mother had been taken ill and died. On her return she was sufficiently miffed at the email and circulated it to her friends, who forwarded it to their friends. The story made the national press and broadcast media. The partner resigned and the law firm's reputation was tarnished. See www.brilliant-email.com for more such examples of email media disasters.

How has email evolved?

Email was designed as a messaging tool, for sending clear, unequivocal, unemotional and preferably short messages. That has not changed in the 30 years it has been around, but what has changed is its accessibility. It is no longer confined to a few boffins or geeks with large computers. Today everyone, everywhere, can use emails at any time to send and exchange information anywhere, from the smallest to largest computer. You don't need permission to send an email as you did in the early days of its use in business. Email software has become more and more sophisticated and feature-rich. However, whatever email software you use (from Notes to Outlook to Googlemail), its core purpose is to be a simple messaging system. This is something most of us forget as we hit 'Send' without giving a thought to the alternatives available to us.

Speed versus depth and breadth of communications

Email is easy, always on and takes little effort. Other options may require more effort and time. With email you get a very blinkered dialogue, whereas even a short conversation often reveals information about other seemingly unrelated, yet often important, topics (a cursory reference to a job vacancy, a way someone else handled a difficult customer, a new competitor, the opportunity for a new story, etc.)

With one client we had an email-free afternoon as part of a major internal campaign to improve efficiency through better use of email. One senior director openly spoke about how, after walking and talking to several colleagues, he had a far greater insight into what people were doing, their workload and the depth and breadth of activities with which his department was involved.

brilliant example

Next time you are about to send an email to someone in your building, stop. Go and talk to them. Note all the other information you glean, not just by talking to that individual but from looking around the office and the corridor conversations that happen en-route. Then make an honest judgement about how much more you have learnt and the value it added to how you do your job and run your team/operation.

Most people quite rightly think that email is quicker and that using the phone can take much longer. For instance, suppose you wanted the opinion of five key colleagues about a short proposal or document. Using email, this might take a maximum of 15 minutes (five to send the email and ten to scan their responses). By phone the minimum is around 30 to 45 minutes – five minutes per person and then at least five minutes to assimilate their comments.

If speed equals productivity, then email wins hands down. But is this the correct way to make a judgement about communications?

Minimising misunderstandings and communicating more accurately

A framework called 'media richness' was developed by Daft and Lengel. The aim was to categorise different communications channels by their ability to allow the sender to communicate information accurately, without it being misunderstood by the recipient. In an age where the norm is email or text messaging, this concept can help you decide when to use alternatives to email.

decide when to use alternatives to email

Based on this, an overview of the current array of ways to communicate is shown in Figure 7.1.

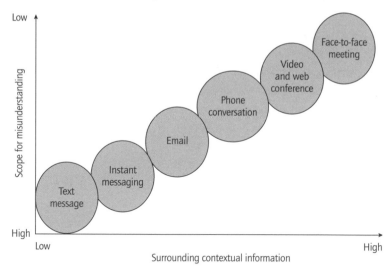

Figure 7.1 Spectrum of communications media

The conclusion was that the more surrounding body language and gestures that accompany a message, the richer and so more easily understood it will be. Therefore, the richer the communication medium, the better it is for conveying complex and emotive messages, especially those easily open to differing interpretations, such as reviewing performance, a lost sale, nego-tiating a deal.

Using a 'rich' communication medium like a face-to-face meeting allows any misunderstandings or misperceptions to be quickly corrected and the communications re-aligned. A simpler or 'lean' medium like text messaging and email has no associated context. Once the message has been received and misinterpreted it can take time to re-align understandings and retrieve a situation.

Additionally, the longer the gap between the misunderstanding and the opportunity to rectify it, the harder it can become to retrieve the situation because the incorrect picture will have become established in the recipient's mind.

Drawing on the 'media richness' framework, here are the three rules of thumb for making decisions and choosing the optimum communications channel:

1 How easy is it for your message to be misunderstood?

2 If your message is misunderstood, how quickly can you get the interaction back on the right track?

3 How much does it matter to you (and your business) if the interaction is misunderstood?

Media richness at work – justifying the choice

A simple medium like email and text messaging is excellent for factual non-emotive messages. These leave no scope for misunder-standing and, even if there were any, there would be no extra cost to you and your business. Ideally you should not sack employees by email, let alone by text message, as this is a very emotive matter.

However, consider this example: in 2009 Hyde Park Corner Autocentre sacked its entire staff by email. Was it easy for the message to be misunderstood? No. Did it matter to the business? No. The company had just ceased trading. Employees were outraged at being sacked by email, feeling it was the wrong medium. The managing director defended his choice of medium by saying 'I wanted to tell everybody at the same time and that [email] was the best thing to do and follow it up with a phone call.' For the sender it worked and the negative consequences were zero. Hence it was probably the most cost-effective choice of media.

While I don't endorse the use of email in such circumstances, do not be put off by headlines like 'Payout for worker sacked by email' and 'Teacher sacked by email'. The case is generally about the cause of and grounds for dismissal rather than the manner.

Nonetheless, where there is scope for misunderstanding, even if the message seems uncontroversial, look for a richer medium as there will be a high cost if it all goes pear-shaped.

Consider this example: you want to take a day's leave. It's the busiest part of the month but your reason is important to you (for example, a friend's wedding). An email message could be misinterpreted as 'I don't care' and the response could be no. There would then be little scope for renegotiating. The optimum channel here would be a conversation, as then you can explain yourself and sell your case better.

Email does have many considerable advantages over other media in the communications spectrum, in particular talking. However, these advantages can quickly become disadvantages if email is used irresponsibly, as the next chapter will demonstrate.

 **brilliant** recap

- Email may be one of the fastest ways to communicate, but in contrast to a conventional face-to-face conversation, email provides a very narrow blinkered dialogue. This means there can be considerable scope for misunderstandings, which can be costly. Other important information can be missed.

- Looking at the 'richness' of the media allows you to evaluate at the broadest level the best choice of communication channels for your message in a given set of circumstances.

- Before defaulting to email ask yourself:

  - Is speed the only consideration?

  - What might be the cost to me (or my business) if there is a major misunderstanding as a result of the recipient not seeing the full picture?

  - Is there a better way(s) to communicate my message that will limit the risk of any major misunderstanding?

  - Does the cost and time of using an alternative outweigh the cost of a misunderstanding?

CHAPTER 8

Email – exploiting advantages and avoiding disadvantages

Be daring, be first, be different, be just.

Anita Roddick

Speed and the number of people who can be quickly reached is email's greatest advantage. But what if you email information to the wrong person or type something in haste you regret? This might mean a breach of confidentiality, sensitive data being leaked, the wrong decision or a lost client. It is very important to recognise when the strength of email may also be its biggest weakness. Appreciating all the attributes of email makes it much easier to choose how to use email to maximum advantage and be more productive. This chapter covers:

- email's strengths and how these can also be its downfall
- recognising the pitfalls of email and their potential cost
- capitalising on the strengths of email, limiting its weaknesses and therefore the cost of misuse
- measures to preserve security and confidentiality when emailing
- deploying a wider range of communications channels to save time communicating.

Strengths and weaknesses of email unravelled

Table 8.1 summarises the key benefits and drawbacks of using email instead of talking – the richest of media and, for many, the best method of communication.

It's not always a black and white decision. It's like trying to decide whether it would be 'greener' and more effective to go by car or by train. Although the train is greener, it could well take longer and be more expensive.

Table 8.1 Strengths and weaknesses of email

Criteria	Strength	Weakness
Quick and fast	✓	✓
Bridges time and location differences	✓	
Carries no body language and sense of context		✓
Provides an audit trail of what was said	✓	✓
Can limit the level of distractions and interruptions	✓	✓
Creates a push rather than pull information culture		✓
Email conversations can quickly spiral out of hand		✓
Provides time and space to craft a reply	✓	
Induces endless chatter in the organisation		✓
Eco-friendly (for example, reduces use of paper)	✓	✓
Enables one to attach files containing supporting information	✓	✓
Encourages creativity		✓
Encourages and allows communications across hierarchies and boundaries	✓	
Lowers the quality of communications		✓
Implies the recipient has taken action		✓
Confidentiality		✓

The following is a review of some of these criteria that will show you how to build on the positives, limit the risks from the negative aspects and when you just have to live with the inherent disadvantages of using email.

Quick and fast

Speed and ease of use is probably email's number one advantage and disadvantage. Once you've hit 'Send' there's no going back, and before you know it an email disaster may have broken out. If your incorrect, misdirected or gossip-laden email leaks beyond your initial recipient, then you and your company could be the stars of the next email media disaster. (Examples of email disasters to avoid can be found at www.brilliant-email.com.)

Another major weakness of email is that we can easily add as many people to the 'Cc' and/or 'To' box as we think might be interested in what we have to say. This massively drives up the volume of email traffic.

> ### brilliant tip
>
> Limiting the volume of emails sent will reduce the volume of emails you receive.

Other ways to reduce the risks of hitting 'Send' too quickly include:

- Read and re-read your message before sending to check that what you've written is what you really meant to say.
- Be ruthless about the number of people you send your message to. Be daring and reduce the total number (both in the 'To' and 'Cc' box) by at least 20 per cent. Invoke the principle of sending only to those who really must know.

always sleep on/ discuss
v. sensitive emails

- When in doubt, save the email in the draft box, have a coffee/sleep on it and re-read it before sending. One executive who uses the draft box principle reckons that about 20 per cent of his emails never actually get sent.
- Delay sending any email for at least two minutes.

---

brilliant example

'The two-minute quarantine rule has saved me, many times, from the consequences of emails that would otherwise have been regretted or recalled. Some would have been sent in error, perhaps through hitting the Send button too early or instead of Save. Others would have been sent in haste, perhaps in the heat of the moment. The two-minute rule buys me a second-chance, and I only wish that functionality extended to emails sent on the BlackBerry.'

Richard Stagg, Editorial Director at Pearson Education

To write such a 'Rule' in Outlook go to 'Tools'/'Rules and Alerts' and from the 'Rules Wizard', pick 'Check messages after sending' (Figure 8.1). Click 'Next' twice (click on 'Yes' to the box asking if the Rule is to be applied to every message) and on the next screen tick the box marked 'defer delivery by a number of minutes'. Then click on the link 'a number of' in Step 2. Select the delay time and click 'Next' to add any exceptions, then 'Finish'.

Bridges the difference in time zones and geographic locations

This is another great advantage of email, especially if you work in a global business, but it is often abused by people who send emails to colleagues in the same building, even those only two desks away. This can have serious financial consequences, as witnessed by the example opposite.

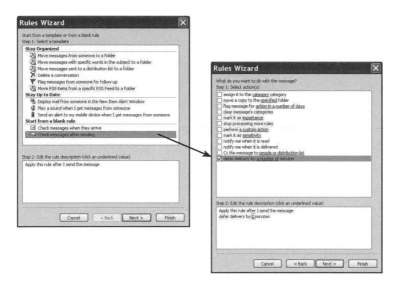

Figure 8.1 Two-minute delay rule for sending emails

 example

A forklift truck driver diligently loaded his lorry one morning only to return to his desk to find an email from his colleague at the next desk about an urgent extra pallet. This had to go on the truck that day but the pallet was in another part of the warehouse. The truck had to be re-loaded from scratch to accommodate the extra palate and the delivery was late. The result was a cross customer who deducted money for the late delivery.

---

brilliant tip

Announce an amnesty on sending emails within a ten-desk radius, and always talk if it's time-critical.

You could also extend the no-email zone to a two-floor radius and thereby improve your fitness and health.

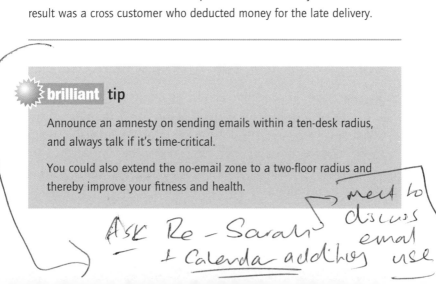

Carries no body language and sense of context

Are you laughing or crying as you send your email? It could be argued that you can insert an emoticon (or smiley) to convey some sense of context and emotions. But beware as it could convey totally the wrong impression.

In a recent workshop, at least 75 per cent of participants cringed and said that smileys convey the exact opposite to that intended. They found them very annoying and said they look 'cheesy' and 'unprofessional' in the work place. The other 25 per cent said they liked them as they 'add a touch of humour' and 'friendship'.

brilliant tip

In business emails, don't even contemplate a smiley. If more 'emotional information or intelligence' needs imparting, compose your message to say what you mean or pick up the phone and talk.

The email audit trail exposed

In today's increasingly litigious society, an audit trail of what has been said and done is often essential. Email can be a double-edged sword. For example, businesses to which the Corporate Manslaughter Act is applicable need to have a record of who told who, what and when. Without such an audit trail it can be difficult to assign responsibility if there is a major incident.

> email can be a double-edged sword

Sadly, the audit trail phenomenon is often used to create a blame culture within organisations about fairly trivial matters. 'I asked you to do X. You did not do it and I have the email to prove it.' X is often neither life threatening nor will it cost the business if it is not done immediately. In many cases a conversation would have been better and more effective. It would have allowed you to see if the other person understood the request and had any intention (never mind the time and inclination) to do X.

---

brilliant dos and don'ts

To minimise the risk of an audit trail becoming more of a disadvantage than an advantage:

Do

- Make a note of the request for yourself and get on: you don't need to send a follow-up email. The exception to this is the classic corridor conversation with a senior executive who you are trying to warm up. Then if asked for an email – do it and make the link to the corridor conversation.

  this works

- Speak when matters are spiralling out of hand before committing words to email.   *Yes → especially with peers*

Don't

- Ever put anything in an email that you are not prepared to defend in court.
- Use an audit for matters which do not carry a cost to the business or require to be audited for compliance, such as ordering pens.
- Respond to a verbal request with 'Put it in an email'.   *I must break this habit*

Push or pull communications culture

One of the reasons many people feel so overloaded and stressed by email is not just the volume, but the fact that it's dumped on them unbidden. This is commonly referred to as a 'push' information culture. Communications are issued regardless of the individual's needs or interest in them. Typical of this syndrome is the blanket 'All users' emails. The top management team decrees what employees need to know. The major pitfall of this system is that each individual can delete these items unopened.

The alternative and healthier culture is a 'Pull' one. It implies that items of potential interest are posted somewhere (generally on the intranet and blogs). You can seek them out when you wish. It's a much less stressful approach and, to a large extent, the holy grail of knowledge management.

> social media is very
> much a 'pull' culture

Social media is very much a 'pull' culture – you choose what you read and when. For a more detailed explanation of push–pull information cultures and how to create them using social media see www.brilliant-email.com.

To move away from push and towards a pull culture:

- Limit the number of 'All user' 'and 'Cc'd' email.
- Use intranets and blogs to distribute blanket information.
- Be selective: ask yourself, 'Who really needs this information?' Use the principle of must know, maybe should know, nice but doesn't really need.

A major benefit of sending out fewer emails is that you will reduce the number of emails you personally receive and your overall email stress levels.

Induces endless chatter in the organisation

It's easy to play endless rounds of 'email thank you', with no one quite knowing when to close the conversation down:

- Stop sending endless pleasantries like 'Thanks', 'My pleasure' and 'OK' – this will reduce the risk of endless empty email conversations.
- Prioritise your information needs and push back unwanted emails (see Chapter 3).

Eco-friendly

Email has the power to drive forward the green economy. Yet many would agree that it has had the reverse effect. For most, the paperless office remains a myth. Look around your own office. Read Sellen and Harper's *The Myth of the Paperless Office*.

To assess how green your workspace is, check:

● How many piles of paper do you see around you?
● How many of these are printouts of emails (or attachments)?
● How many email-enabled devices are running and driving up the level of electricity consumed?
● Of these email-enabled devices, how many do you really need going at one time?
● By how much has your demand for storage space increased as a result of the volume of email traffic?

Common retorts to the last question are that 'Storage is cheap', 'It's in the cloud', 'It's unlimited'. All true but, however energy-efficient, these servers are still driven by electricity.

To enable email to support the green economy:

● Reduce the level of email traffic and amount of emails kept and especially in archive (.pst) files.
● Be daring and talk more.
● Avoid the trap of following up conversations with an email unless the matter is contractual. If it is, the email can be shorter as it need only be a summary of the agreed points.

The managing director of one international management accountancy firm recently asked his business systems team to provide a solution to the current paper and energy burn being generated by the increase in email storage systems. It's a work in progress, and a total ban on using .pst files are some of the options now being considered.

Lowers the quality of communications

A recent survey by the DTI suggested that email can lower the quality of communications because of the sloppy ways in which people write emails and include jokes and other casual remarks. For more on this, see Chapter 13. Email allows one to get away with sloppy communications, especially those sent from a hand-held device such as a BlackBerry or iPhone.

Shipley and Schwalbe (2007) suggest that to include the strapline 'Sent from my BlackBerry' acts almost as an acceptable apology for sloppy communications. Indeed, some users even add to the BlackBerry line with 'Small keyboard, big thumbs' asking for mistakes to be excused. What's your view? These communications will affect your image so you must decide on the best course of action for your business.

To improve the quality of email communications:

● Decide what is best for you and your business: speed of response or slower response and better quality communications.

● For those managing businesses, check your email best practice policy for guidelines on email and compliance. Chapter 17 has more about this.

An email sent can imply the recipient has taken action

The biggest problem in communications is the illusion that it has taken place.

George Bernard Shaw

A common mistake. As seen in Chapter 1, many people read emails but actually then do nothing with them. Do not rely on either the email-read receipt or delivery receipt as confirmation that any action will be taken. Moreover, read receipts can smack of playing politics and make people feel even more like ignoring you.

brilliant tip

Ask for a reply as confirmation of the recipient's intentions or follow up during the day with a conversation. This reduces the risk of sending an email only to find the recipient takes no action.

Confidentiality

This is a major challenge and in many respects has nothing to do with the richness of the media used. An email is no more confidential than a postcard. There are three key reasons. First, anyone with access to the email server can read the content of an email if they are minded too, as illustrated by this example.

brilliant example

In 2008, an IT technician at the Body Shop was fined £850,000 for accessing confidential email which contained information about the state of Body Shop sales. He used the information to short the stock and bet on their share price falling.

Second, you think you have sent the email to the right Dave Smith but what happens if you haven't? How many times have you had a message to the effect 'Ignore last (and confidential) email' message? Worse still is the 'Sender wishes to recall this email'. We are all nosy and by the time the second email comes through most of us have opened the first one and seen something we really should not have done.

Third is the compromising situation in which you send a highly sensitive and confidential email to someone only to discover their PA is managing their inbox and sees it. Now you have compromised both yourself and possibly the PA. I conducted a survey across 300 PAs and administrators that revealed that 82 per cent had accidentally read confidential information at one time or another. While most managers would say their PA is the most trusted person in their business lives, there are still occasions when either they should not or do not want to see highly sensitive information.

→ GM as Head, I want control of
my inbox.
Not via a PA

🌟 brilliant dos and don'ts

There are several ways to reduce the risk of breaching confidentiality through email.

Do

● Mark the email confidential and warn the recipient if talking is not possible. As a recipient, use a 'Rule' to move all such emails to a folder which only you access and read.

● Turn off the auto-address feature.

● Send the information as a password-protected attachment – this cannot be seen by anyone checking in the mail server room.

● Encrypt the email if that option is available to you.

Don't

● Use email – talk. Of course there is still nothing to stop the other person gossiping, but at least you have some control of the initial delivery of the information.

Attributes of email and media richness

These key attributes of email and their relationship to the richness of the medium are summarised in Figure 8.2. Use the summary as a quick reference template for assessing the optimum communication choice. Review the criteria listed and add others as appropriate to your situation.

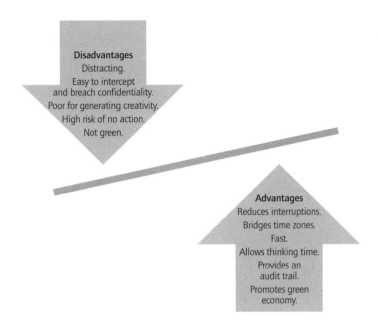

Figure 8.2 Advantages and disadvantages of email

Benefits of using the full range of communications channels

Precision of communication is important, more important than ever, in our era of hair-trigger balances, when a false or misunderstood word may create as much disaster as a sudden thoughtless act.

James Thurber

The downside of using 'richer' communications channels than email is that they generally take longer. A blog takes more time to write. Videoconferencing often means pre-booking the technology – although increasingly people now have Skype. Discussions with several contributors to this book were done through Skype, and the ability to see their faces greatly enhanced the quality of the discussion and helped build relationships.

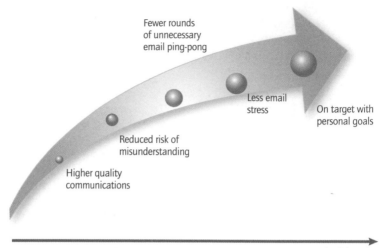

Fewer rounds
of unnecessary
email ping-pong

Less email
stress

On target with
personal goals

Reduced risk of
misunderstanding

Higher quality
communications

Productivity gains

Figure 8.3 Benefits of using a wider range of communications channels

The upside is that widening your range and choice of communications media will enable you to save time and improve your own productivity, as summarised in Figure 8.3.

In addition, using a broader and richer range of communications provides opportunities to:

● widen the scope of the discussion and pick up useful information about other potential opportunities

● limit breaches of confidentiality

● develop a better understanding of related issues which might impinge on the business.

The goal of any communication should be 'right message right first time'. This can only be attained through being selective about which channel you use and when.

brilliant recap

- Email software is feature-rich. Nonetheless, email remains a thin medium that lacks the ability to convey any of the associated contextual and emotional information surrounding the message.

- Be more selective and daring in the channels you use.

- Here are seven ways to leverage the potential of email and mitigate the downsides of it being – at times – too easy and fast:

    1   Limit your use of email to simple factual messages. Choose a richer medium such as talking for complex, emotional messages, especially when there is a significant chance of a misunderstanding which could put you and your business at risk.

    2   Be very selective about who you include in 'All user' and 'Cc' emails.

    3   If things go pear-shaped, talk. Don't default to the email audit trail, which is often only the symptom not the problem.

    4   Reduce the level of email stress by creating a 'pull' rather than a 'push' information culture – for example, posting general information on intranets in preference to sending 'All user' emails.

    5   Don't assume a sent message will either be opened or actioned. Where action is needed, especially if it's urgent, talk first and email later.

    6   Take adequate steps to reduce the risk of leaking confidential information.

    7   Write a 'Rule' to delay sending any email by at least two minutes.

Handwritten annotations: "Re panels", "Speak more by phone + in meetings", "interesting → explore..."

CHAPTER 9

When to email and when to talk

Email is not a discussion.

Marsha Egan, author of *Inbox Detox*

I n this chapter we apply the pros and cons of email to help you choose when to email and when to pick an alternative way to communicate your message. Some common everyday tasks are reviewed to see how you can save time by choosing the best medium, which might not always be email.

To email or not to email?

Table 9.1 gives an overview of some typical day-to-day tasks and what might be the most productive way to communicate. Many people say phoning is not a good option as people often don't answer their phone. Nonetheless, a phone message can sometimes convey much more warmth and sincerity than an email or text message.

Table 9.1 To email or not to email – what is most effective?

Task/activity	Best choice
Arranging a meeting	Internally – calendar invite/scheduler – not email ping-pong. Externally look to share your calendar.
Send meeting papers	As an attachment in a separate email, rather than attaching files to the meeting invite.

▶

Table 9.1 *continued*

Task/activity	Best choice
Performance feedback	Conversation – never by email.
Sale (to new or existing client)	Warm up by email and close by conversation.
Negotiation needing delicate buy-in (for example, discount, change project deadline, move staff)	Conversation.
Shortlist applications for job	Email.
Advise of offer/rejection	Email or letter.
Send information (for example, article, sales figures, budgets, legal advice, CVs)	Email (perhaps as an attachment, depending on length).
Delegating a simple task (for example, order train ticket, fix golf tee time)	Email.
Delegate complex task (for example, arrange/change of council housing)	Conversation backed up by an email.
Thanks for excellence/special effort	Handwritten note/postcard
Following up after an incident	Conversation.
Agree a contract/changes to a contract	Email or letter (depending on your business).
Social trivia (cakes for tea, etc.)	Instant messaging (otherwise an email with an expiry date).
Who knows about …	Email to a selected cohort likely to have an answer – not the whole company.
Internal business news (of all types from annual figures to new joiners)	Intranet/blog/wikis (at best an email with a link to the intranet).
Gossip and jokes	Conversation only, never by email.

Some of the above warrant further explanation, as it is not always clear cut which medium will enable you to communicate the 'right message right first time'. All examples are drawn from real instances which people have come up against in their pursuit of email excellence to improve productivity, for themselves and their business.

Arranging a meeting

[handwritten: All my teaching + other commitments uploaded]

Arranging meetings is one of those tasks which most of us, espe-cially PAs, would say takes a disproportionate amount of time.

 brilliant timesaver

> A major government department estimates it saved 80,000 working hours by making it mandatory for all staff to keep their calendar current and to always arrange a meeting using the calendar scheduling function rather than through email ping-pong.

[handwritten: discuss w/ Sarah]

Make it personal (and business) policy to maintain a current calendar which, at the minimum, shows when you are free, away, or have a tentative meeting. Always include travel time if the meeting is away from the office. This saves confusion and time when meetings need re-arranging once someone realises that they need an extra hour to travel.

Playing email ping-pong to arrange meetings is probably one of the biggest timewasters, especially for PAs and executive assist-ants. Other ways to save time arranging meetings include:

● Using an online calendar.

● Outlook 2007 users can email an external person their calendar (or an extract of it).

● Outlook users (all versions) can use 'Voting' buttons if you are looking for a forced choice, i.e. one date only. Voting buttons are great timesavers as they correlate responses automatically (like the meeting request function).

To share your calendar by email, switch to 'Calendar View' and, from the 'Current View' panel, pick 'Send a calendar via email' (Figure 9.1). This creates a blank email. Select the date ranges from the dialogue box and click OK. Your calendar is then dropped into the email.

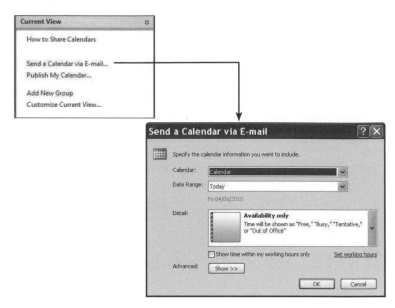

Figure 9.1 Send your calendar by email

To insert a voting button, open a new email and click on the 'Options' tab/'More options' – the right-hand arrow – and then type in your options as shown in Figure 9.2.

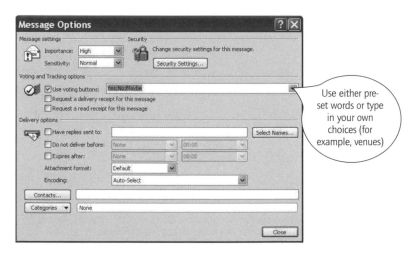

Figure 9.2 Voting buttons

Administrators and PAs are always asking for tips on how to save time and avoid endless email exchanges when setting up internal or external meetings.

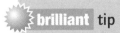 **timesaver**

This is the timesaving process one major international consultancy house uses for arranging meetings, especially when participants come from different time zones.

- Agree who essential participants are.
- Agree who can least and most be inconvenienced by changes in time zones.
- Arrange a conference call with all the relevant PAs and administrators to decide a date and venue.
- Then, and only then, send out the meeting invites.

Performance feedback

Giving feedback to anyone (from colleague to external supplier) should initially always be done by discussion, whether by phone or in person. There are always two sides to a story. Once you commit to print (or, in this case, email) the die is cast and an email war could start. With external suppliers it is important to remember that they may also supply your clients. You could easily find your reputation damaged by idle comments about how you handled them.

brilliant tip

Talk first, then email second to confirm what was agreed.

Sales and negotiations

Email makes it easy for your recipient to ignore you and even close you out. Supposing you are trying to sell an extra printer or magazine feature, or negotiate an extra discount. Once the recipient has said no it's hard to re-open the door. Try and the result is often ignored emails and phone calls. Talking takes more time but you glean so much more information – when might be the next opportunity to talk, what else is going on, why, etc.

> **it's hard to re-open the door**

Email is a great tool during a sale or ongoing negotiations as you can send hard factual information and arrange follow-up calls. But don't use it to close a sale or clinch negotiations.

brilliant example

One client who had just been recruited as a fundraising manager was quite rightly constantly phoning potential donors. Then his colleagues complained about the noise! His solution was to keep talking, but find a free room in which to work.

When does a simple task become complex?

A common question is 'What sort of tasks/requests can easily be actioned by email?' Basically the answer is, anything simple that will not require endless email exchanges before clarity and agreement is reached.

The key to keeping the request simple and reducing email exchanges is thinking ahead (both as recipient and sender), as illustrated by this example.

brilliant example

A footwear supplier contacted its Hong Kong manufacturer to complain about an order. When the manufacturer asked for clarification about what was wrong with the colour and shape of the bow, the reply came: 'A little more pink and squarer.'

It took about eight rounds of email exchanges to get to the correct order because no one thought ahead about what other data might be needed. Each email exchange was just a series of monosyllabic answers, such as 'Darker pink', 'Smaller square', 'It's urgent' and so on. Eventually the complete picture emerged: 'Pantone number 214 and bow shape 301. Order must be included in Thursday shipment for Client D.'

There were some language barriers. Nonetheless the supplier was an experienced buyer and knew that all the data given in the 'big picture' might be needed; this could easily have been included in the original request to the Hong Kong office. This would have saved everyone time, reduced the level of frustration and maintained profit margins. In this example, the manufacturer missed the shipping deadline (as often happened because of poor use of email), so the shoes often had to be sent by air rather than ship. This reduced the profit margin by at least 50 per cent.

brilliant tip

Before you send an email asking someone a question (or asking them to take action), put yourself in their shoes and think ahead.

Before hitting 'Send', ask yourself what other supporting information will the recipient need. Ask 'What will be their response?' Try to pre-empt it in your first email by including any additional information they might ask for.

The task may be as simple as producing this week's sales figures, drafting a response to a client question, or ordering more flip-chart paper, but if you don't include the context, you leave yourself open to playing endless time-wasting rounds of email ping-pong. Always endeavour to include specifics such as how many, what size, shape, product specifications, location, deadlines, non-negotiable boundaries like method of transport, cost, etc.

always endeavour to include specifics

This will greatly reduce the risk of a simple task turning into a seemingly complex one through endless email exchanges. That said, there will always be some email exchanges where you just have to talk and agree a way forward.

brilliant tip

When you have played three rounds of email ping-pong and the matter is no nearer closure, it's time to talk.

Is it OK to say 'Thank you' or 'Well done' by email?

How many of you have certificates and trophies, etc., on your desk? These are tangible acknowledgements of tasks well done or excellence. They would not work so well as an email printout. However, email thank yous and recognitions of excellence are nonetheless much appreciated and should still be sent, but perhaps consider the value of sending a handwritten postcard in addition or instead.

Many successful business leaders have a stock of postcards in their top drawer for just such occasions. A handwritten note still conveys a much deeper sense of praise and gratitude, perhaps because it does take a few minutes longer than an email. Handwritten notes raise your profile in the eyes of the recipient and are a good way to build relationships and motivation, espe-cially with team members.

Following up after an incident

This could be the subject of a book in itself. The key point to remember here is the richer the medium of communication, the greater the perceived level of sincerity. That's why in a crisis a personal appearance, face-to-face meeting, phone call or voice message will convey a much greater level of genuineness.

 **example**

At the Trafford Centre if there is ever an incident (for example, a visitor is taken ill), the Customer Service Manager always telephones the next day to ask how the person feels. If there is no reply he leaves a voice message. Their rationale is that a voice message conveys a much warmer and caring tone than an email (or even a letter).

Agree a contract/changes to a contract

There are no rights or wrongs. Just bear in mind these points:

- The content of an email is legal and can be used as evidence in court.
- Email encourages speedy responses, whereas writing takes time but allows you space to think and organise your thoughts.
- Letters (even as attachments) convey a more professional image.

ve HM newsletter.

For the last reason, many companies still require a 'wet signa-ture' – i.e. a letter – for matters relating to changes in contractual matters. The use of email for contractual matters may be dic-tated to you by your business. If you are the owner, ask yourself:

- Is speed of the essence?

- What is the risk to my business of using email in terms of not giving myself (or my colleagues) time to think things through thoroughly?

- What image does contracting by email convey?

In our business we make it a principle always to follow up an agreement with a short letter (albeit attached to an email) outlining what's been agreed, what will be delivered, by when and at what cost. The letter also always contains our terms and conditions.

Social trivia

For those who have instant messaging, portals with news areas, and any other form of real-time social networking facility, this is the best place to communicate all the office social stuff, like 'Cakes for my birthday', 'Can anyone lend me a phone charger?', 'The sandwich man is here in reception', etc.

This is the quickest way to reduce the volume of non-core email and reduce the storage capacity needed for email. Have no doubt there are many who don't do mailbox housekeeping and leave all such messages in their inbox to be archived by whatever means.

Who knows about …

The classic timewaster in law practices is when money arrives and it's not clear to which account it belongs. Usually an 'All user' email is sent. In seconds a PA will answer to identify the owner and out goes another message – 'Disregard the first email'. What a waste of time and server capacity. To compound matters, any PA looking after a partner's mailbox then has to delete all the messages from their partner's inbox as well as their own. Time could be saved by using a selected email distribution list or instant messaging. If that does not yield the answer, only then use the 'All user' email route. Eight out of ten times one of the former will work for whatever is being requested.

Internal business news

In workshops, seven out of ten people usually comment on internal newsletters and how they rarely read them but cannot unsubscribe from the distribution list. A high percentage (in some cases at least 60 per cent) are deleted unopened. How much time and energy is being wasted?

As indicated in Chapter 8, intranets, portals and social media provide people and business with one of the most powerful and cost-effective ways to communicate more effectively while reducing the volume of unnecessary emails and energy costs.

Love affairs, gossip and jokes

Keep these for chatting at the vending machine or water fountain. Never, ever put these in a business email. It takes years to build a good reputation and brand image. A careless email can destroy it in a nanosecond. There are countless tales of boy or girl tells friend what he/she did that night and, before you can blink, emails are out all over the internet and you and your organisation are the stars of the next email media disaster. In some cases such as Harry Stonecipher, CEO of Boeing, it cost the company dearly as their share price plummeted. For examples of such email disasters see www.brilliant-email.com.

How you use your personal email account is your personal affair. Your business email address belongs to the company and as such is governed by the business's policy. By and large these usually stipulate no jokes and the like. If you are not sure what your policy says and what the repercussions of a breach are, check it now before it's too late.

If you have any doubts that you can keep an office affair private when you use the business email, read Lucy Kellaway's *In Office Hours*.

 **recap**

- When you have played email ping-pong more than three times and the matter is still not resolved – talk.

- Think before hitting 'Send' and ask yourself what other information might the recipient need from you to be able to answer your email. Then include that in your email.

- Use instant messaging for all non-essential (social) type conversations which do not and need not form part of an auditable part of the business.

- Keep the gossip and the jokes for the coffee machine.

- Don't use business email for matters relating to your love life.

- Use the calendar scheduler to arrange a meeting but send the meeting papers in a separate email.

- Consider making a phone call. A voice message still carries tone and is warmer than an email message.

- Keep a collection of postcards in your top drawer for acknowledging special performances.

- Limit your distribution list to those who really really need to know. Post on intranets and blog information which others might find useful.

- Avoid using email during delicate stages of a sale/negotiation – it makes it too easy for the recipient to shut you out and close the door on the sale/negotiation.

Create excellent emails

'As the volume of communications via email increases, we need to differentiate ourselves, make our voices heard, cut through the noise.'

John Freeman, *The Tyranny of E-mail.*

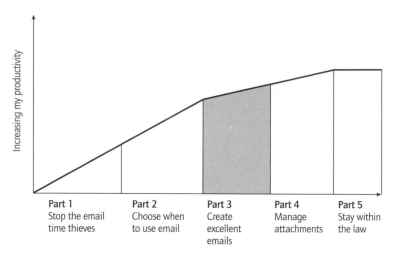

Five steps to improving my productivity – create excellent emails

Part Three covers how to create an excellent email that increases productivity by conveying the right message right first time.

There are five elements to an excellent email that will help you stand out from the crowd and constitute your 'email dress code'.

1   Subject line – eye-catching.

2   Address box – correct use of 'To' and 'Cc' lines.

3   Greeting – draw the recipient in.

4   Content – crystal clear to convey your message immediately.

5   Sign off and signature – impeccable and easy for the recipient to contact you.

Should an email be as perfect as a letter?

This question is posed frequently by clients, of all ages, all sectors and from business of all sizes. Some argue that email is an informal communication and that more lax rules, grammar, punctuation and layout are acceptable. However, for most of us, email is our primary form of business communication. It sends a signal about you and your business just as clearly as the clothes you wear send a message about you and your persona.

More often than not, you and your email recipient will not have met, let alone spoken. But within ten seconds of reading your email the recipient will have formed a picture of you and it may not be the one you wanted to convey. Nonetheless, it is their picture and it determines the tenor of the relationship. Sloppy email reflects badly on you because it suggests both you and your business are sloppy.

It doesn't hurt to say

Your email must therefore instantly convey the right tone and language. This must be carried through from the initial greeting to your signature and disclaimer at its end if you want to convey a professional image.

"Dear X"

Well crafted emails save time because they convey the right message immediately. This means no wasted time reading and re-reading emails and playing email ping-pong, trying to understand what is being said. The following chapters will show you how to optimise the use of each of the five elements of your email dress code to make your emails stand out, and further leverage the timesaving advice in Parts 1 and 2.

brilliant tip

To benchmark the overall quality of your emails at any time, go to www.brilliant-email.com and use the 'Email Clarity' benchmarking tool.

CHAPTER 10

Get your email noticed

Today, communication itself is the problem. We have become the world's first over-communicated society. Each year we send more and receive less.

Al Rie

In any email management workshop the quality of the subject line (or the lack of it) is among the first five most annoying issues cited by participants. How often have you wasted time opening an email only to find that the content bore no relation to the subject line? This chapter covers:

- How to write eye-catching subject lines that immediately gain the recipient's attention and point out the email's purpose, saving you both time.

- How to edit the subject line in emails from others to help yourself be more productive and influence others to change.

- Timesaving software functions to enable you to make even better use of the subject line.

- The benefits of writing good subject lines.

The subject line of an email is like a news headline. It should draw your attention to that specific story or email. A good subject line helps you decide if the email is relevant and

the subject line of an email is like a news headline

should be prioritised for action. The need for high quality subject lines is magnified today, as so many people now pick up their emails on a handheld device with a small screen.

For those using electronic document management systems and archiving solutions, subject lines also act as a tag by which the email can be automatically sorted and archived for future use.

What makes an excellent subject line?

 brilliant timesaver

Brilliant emailers always use accurate, well crafted subject lines that grab the recipient's attention and reflect exactly what is expected from them.

What do the following subject lines tell you?

- Meeting
- Jane's laptop
- Article for Economist

Trawl through your sent items and count how many of your emails have subject lines like these. Do you think they stand out in the recipient's inbox amid the 70 or more other emails they received that day? Little wonder a common challenge is to get people to notice and answer your emails.

 brilliant definition

Subject line

States exactly what the email is about, and what action (if any) is required from the recipient and by when.

There are three elements to a perfect subject line:

1 What level of action is expected from the receiver (action, approval, read, etc.)?

2 Timescale for any expected action.

3 Description of about ten words which tells you exactly what the email is about and matches the content of the email.

Figure 10.1 shows some examples of excellent subject lines designed to stand out and grab the recipient's attention.

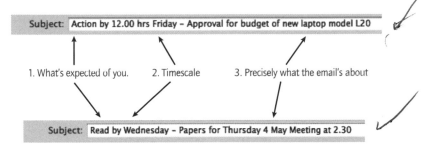

Figure 10.1 Perfect subject lines

Useful abbreviations to signpost the purpose of your email

There are a number of commonly accepted abbreviations which you can use to indicate the purpose of your email (Table 10.1). These help the recipient prioritise their emails and saves you both wasting time playing email ping-pong. Share these with your colleagues and add your own.

EOM (end of message) is really useful for one-line emails: for example, sending a file, passing on a phone message, telling of a change of meeting venue.

Beginning or end of the subject line

The guideline is anything which indicates a level of action should go at the beginning, such as TC, FR, FYI. Although FYI

Table 10.1 Useful abbreviations for subject lines

Abbreviation	Signpost	Beginning or end of line
EOM	End of message – all I have to say is in the subject line	End
FR	For reading	Beginning
FYI	For your information	Beginning
MI	Meeting information	Beginning
NRE	No reply expected	End
TC	Time critical	Beginning

implies no action is required, it is useful at the start to signal just that. Abbreviations which indicate closure go at the end.

Using a combination of FYI and NRE, a good subject line would be:

FYI – Promo shares article for Economist 4 Sep – NRE

Long subject lines can also be hard to see in full on handheld email devices, which is another reason why it's important to put the action notification at the start.

Is it polite to tell people that they don't need to reply?

How often have you replied to an email simply because you are not sure if the sender expects an acknowledgement? This is another source of wasted time which can easily be stopped. Anything that cuts down the number of unnecessary email exchanges is good practice.

brilliant tip

Start using NRE and see how much that reduces the number of unnecessary replies.

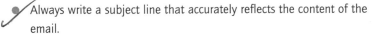 **brilliant** dos and don'ts

Do

- Always write a subject line that accurately reflects the content of the email.

- Update and edit the subject line as the conversation changes. For instance, in the case of an email initially asking for budget approval for a new laptop, after the budget has been approved, update the next email's subject line to read: 'FYI – new laptop model abc will arrive Monday NRE'.

- Tell the recipient precisely what you expect from them and by when.

- Confine the subject line to ten words (plus any project numbers). Any longer and it's *War and Peace*!

- Say if no response/action is expected, using one of the sets of commonly used abbreviations in Table 10.1.

- When forwarding an email, edit the subject line as appropriate to reflect what is needed of the new recipient.

- Many businesses assign unique identifiers (code numbers) to each project/case. Always include these in the subject line. It makes it easier for filing and archiving. For example, 'JKL123 Action by 3.00 pm Thursday – approve revised specification for Room 112'.

- Check your business process guidelines about the applicability of such identification codes and if they must go at the start or end of the subject line. Many businesses have electronic document management systems which automatically link an email to other electronic files. If yours do, it's imperative that the identification number is in the subject line. Otherwise emails cannot always be linked automatically and you might be left to do this manually – another source of unnecessary time wasted.

Don't

- Start a new conversation using an old subject line. For example, take the previous discussion about purchasing a new laptop. If you reply to

▶

the last email, starting a new email thread about a meeting, this makes it hard for the recipient to spot the necessity to prioritise. They probably think the laptop thread is closed. I have missed course bookings when people reply to my emailed newsletter instead of sending a new email as requested!

Send an email with a blank subject line. This looks unprofessional and sloppy. It wastes everyone's time as it is harder to search/file on a blank subject line.

Blank or meaningless subject lines

You have to lead people gently towards what they already know is right.

Philip Crosby

You can easily edit the subject line to a more meaningful one which makes it easier for you to file and find.

In Outlook either open the email and from the 'Other Actions' menu, select 'Edit message' and change the subject line. Click 'Yes' to save changes when closing the email. Alternatively, make the subject line editable *in situ*. This is covered in Chapter 1.

Furthermore, if you edit the subject line when replying, you send a loud message to the original sender about best practice and how to make it easier for you both to sort your emails.

Can I add a reminder to emails I send that need action?

Most email software allows you to add a reminder flag which will jog the recipient at the appropriate time (set by you). You need to judge how this will be perceived by the recipient. In general it is preferable to remind them in person. When this is not possible, inserting a flag can be useful. In Outlook this can be done by clicking on the flag icon when composing a new message.

What about priority markers and read receipts?

Avoid all attention-seeking markers such as high priority markers (the red exclamation mark) and read and delivery receipts. Generally these are perceived as annoying, convey an image of pomposity, create an air of mistrust and can generate even more unnecessary email traffic as the receipts come back into your mailbox and need to be filed or deleted.

brilliant tip

Use read receipts and high priority markers as the exception rather than the norm.

Experience suggests that the worst offenders are senior managers and their PAs who think that their emails are the most important. They insert high priority markers on all email communications. Continuous use of such attention-seeking markers makes it very hard to judge when an email truly is top priority.

Remember that receiving an email read receipt does not necessarily mean it has been properly read and understood, or that it will be actioned.

brilliant tip

If you do work with people who persist in using read receipts, and/ or mark their emails as high priority, ask them why they do it.

Rather than ignoring and/or deleting read receipts, etc., try to address the reasons why the sender feels they need to exhibit such poor email behaviour. Sometimes the sender simply does not realise (or has forgotten) that they turned on these functions on a permanent rather than one-off basis.

Used as an exception rather than the rule, high priority markers and read receipts can be very useful. They alert the recipient that something needs dealing with as a higher than normal priority. Typical examples include:

● Follow-up email about payment.

● Sending out new rotas.

● Emails containing information where there may be a legal liability and/or you need proof of sending. (For example, asking someone to delete emails that are no longer relevant but which, if kept, would be in breach of the Data Protection Act, such as CVs of unsuccessful job applicants or emails relating to sick leave once the person has recovered.)

● Request for removal of equipment, especially where there will be additional costs incurred if notification is not received. (For example, exhibition stands, building equipment, hire cars.)

Expiry dates

For Outlook users, this is a hidden gem. It enables you to set a shelf-life on your emails which in effect tells the recipient not to bother with your email. After the expiry date the email is greyed out in the recipient's mailbox. Expiry dates are great for all those time-specific emails, for example:

● 'No access to the building this weekend.'

● 'Fire alarm is being tested today.'

● 'Remember to complete your timesheets by 5.00 pm.'

● 'Thursday's golf match.'

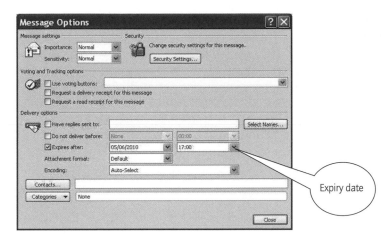

Figure 10.2 Expiry date

And of course – if you must send them – all those celebration cake emails!

To insert an expiry date when writing a new email in Outlook, go to the 'Options' tab/click on the bottom-right arrow. In the 'Delivery options', click on 'Expires after' and select your date (Figure 10.2).

 **brilliant** recap

The subject line is the beacon of your email. It makes it stand out and draws the recipient's eye to it.

● A brilliant subject line increases everyone's productivity because it:

   – greatly improves the likelihood of the recipient spotting your email and actioning it appropriately

   – significantly reduces unnecessary email responses

   – speeds up the filing and linking of an email to other associated files.

● These are the five attributes that every subject line should contain:

   – What action, if any, is required?

▶

- By when this action is needed.
- Ten-word concise description of the email's content.
- Project identification number if appropriate.
- Indication when no response is expected.

● For ongoing email threads, update the descriptive part of the subject to reflect changes in the content.

● High priority alerts, read receipts and reminders are valuable tools when used in moderation.

● Outlook users should include an expiry date on all emails that have a defined shelf-life.

CHAPTER 11

The right
address box

A sheet of carbon paper is sandwiched between two sheets of paper and the pressure applied by the writing implement (pen, pencil, typewriter) to the top sheet causes pigment from the carbon paper to make a similar mark on the copy. More than one copy can be made by stacking several sheets with carbon paper between each pair. The top sheet is the original and each of the additional sheets is called a **carbon copy** *(cc).*

Wikipedia

Have you ever:

- missed an important piece of information or a deadline because an email was not addressed directly to you?
- found it hard to see in which address box your name appears because there are so many names, with the result that you de-prioritise the email and park for attention later?

Intimately linked to the subject line is the address box in which your recipients' names appear ('To', 'Cc' or 'Bcc'). Together these distinguish your email from the multitude of others received during the day. This chapter covers:

- business rules of engagement for the correct use of 'To', 'Cc' and 'Bcc'
- benefits of using the right address box.

Putting the recipient's name in the correct address box is yet another way to save both you and your recipients time and reduce email overload.

Which address line to use – 'To' or 'Cc'?

Many people filter their incoming email on the basis of the address line in which their name appears. They look first and foremost at those emails where they are in the 'To' box. In some cases they only look at emails which are addressed directly to them and never at 'Cc'd' mail, as illustrated by this executive.

---

brilliant example

I often receive over one hundred emails a day. I have a 'Rule' that sends any email where my name is in the 'Cc' box to a separate folder, which I check only when I have time. That might be only once a week.

Business Support Executive, European government department

The accepted rules for business are that if you put the person's name in the:

● 'To' box = action is expected – either to read a document or actively respond.

● 'Cc' box = it's for their information only – you are not expecting them to respond.

Adhering to this convention for 'To' and 'Cc' means you don't waste time chasing up responses from people you accidentally put in the 'Cc' box. Conversely, if your name is in the 'Cc' box, you should not waste your time replying unless it's absolutely essential.

To reduce further the scope for misunderstandings and unnecessary rounds of email ping-pong, consider too adopting the following practices.

brilliant dos and don'ts

Do

- State exactly from whom you expect action (all, just one person, etc.), when including more than one person in the 'To' box. Otherwise, either everyone takes action or no one does as each will assume it is someone else's responsibility.
- Use the 'Bcc' box when emailing more than ten people.

Don't

- 'Reply All' if you are in the 'Cc' box. If you do feel you need to comment, then send your reply only to the sender. (Using 'Reply All' smacks of playing politics. Let the sender decide if everyone needs to see your comments.)

What about the 'Bcc' (Blind carbon copy) box?

How many emails do you receive in which more space is taken up with the list of other names (in the 'To' and/or 'Cc' box) than the content? Typical are the one-liners saying 'Agenda attached for next meeting'.

brilliant example

One person in an international business sent out new product information to a large list containing the names of all their distributors and suppliers. All the names were in the 'Cc' box and thus revealed to everyone on the list sensitive information about who their other distributors were. This one did not make the national press: for others which did, see www.brilliant-email.com.

Disasters can be avoided by using the 'Bcc' box

The 'Bcc' box is a powerful tool for sending emails to many people because everyone on the list sees only their own name. You can use it for lists of names which would appear in either the 'To' or 'Cc' boxes. Using the 'Bcc' box in this way is very effective because it:

● shuts the 'Reply All' floodgate – anyone who does hit 'Reply All' (by accident or deliberately) can send it only to the original sender

● reduces any risk of professional embarrassment from disclosure, i.e. revealing who are the other interested parties

● makes it easy to see your own name as it's not lost in a mass of others

● reduces your carbon footprint by cutting down on wasted space (and paper) from long lists of names in the 'To' and 'Cc' boxes

● keeps you on the right side of the Data Protection Act. Your email address book contacts are personal pieces of information which you must not share with others unless you have their permission.

brilliant tip

When you do use the 'Bcc' box, put your name in the 'To' line and everyone else's in the 'Bcc' box. Start the email with 'Dear/Hi All' and continue as normal. Everyone will know you have used the 'Bcc' box but you reap the advantages just outlined and minimise the confusion and time wasted from too many names in the 'To' or 'Cc' box.

The 'Bcc' box minefield

An obvious assumption is to use the 'Bcc' box when you do want secretly to keep someone in the loop. Well, don't. This perpetuates the blame culture. And it's not too hard as a recipient to work out if others have been Bcc'd in on what seems like a private email exchange.

this perpetuates the blame culture

In Outlook you can use colour to highlight all emails sent only to you. Look carefully at those you think were to you but are not highlighted: it suggests a name in the 'Bcc' box. Sometimes this can be an innocent (albeit poor) use by the recipient – they have put themselves in the 'Bcc' box so the original email re-appears in their inbox as a reminder to them.

 **brilliant** recap

Putting the recipient's name in the right address line is yet another way to be more productive. It saves unnecessary email trails and, in some cases, professional embarrassment.

Adhere to the business standards of using:

● 'To' when you expect action from the recipient.

● 'Cc' for information only.

● 'Bcc' when it would be more prudent not to disclose who are the other recipients.

CHAPTER 12

Greetings to engage recipients

I can feel the twinkle of his eyes in his handshake.

Helen Keller

Why people start an email with no greeting is one of the unsolved mysteries of the internet age. The greeting is the opening handshake of email dialogue. You would never pick up the phone without saying something like 'Hello, this is XXX how are you?' What you say or do not say immediately sets the tone and lays the foundation for the working relationship and probability of doing further business together.

Invite people to read your email

This chapter covers the third and often overlooked component of your brilliant email dress code, the opening greeting. The way you 'invite' people to read your email conveys key information about you and the way you work or interact with people.

 **example**

Example 1

To: Carol Black

From: John Brown

Subject: Budget for meeting with PR agency on Monday at 3.00pm

Where's the briefing for next week's meeting?

JB

Example 2

To: Carol Black

From: John Brown

Subject: Budget for meeting with PR agency on Monday at 3.00pm

Hi Carol,

When will the budget briefing be ready for next week's meeting with the new PR agency?

Regards,

John

Which one of the examples above will generate a more timely and willing response? Probably the second email. It conveys some personalisation, sincerity, warmth and respect. Whereas the first feels like it is almost shouting a command at Carol. It suggests that John is far too busy and possibly too senior to take the time to bother about how to get the best from Carol.

Take time to be polite

I don't want to be sexist here, but some research I undertook a couple of years ago to identify if men and women had different email styles showed that men are more liable to do away with the greetings in email than women.

> it does not take much longer to add a short greeting

They tend to launch straight into the purpose of their email and generally write shorter, more monosyllabic emails. While I applaud trying to keep their time on email to a minimum, it does not take much longer to add a short greeting in keeping with their relationship with the recipient.

Greet the recipient as you would want to be greeted. Here are some ways to greet people by email.

⚡ brilliant dos and don'ts

Do

- Always use one of the following to greet the recipient: 'Dear', 'Hello', 'Hi', 'Good morning/evening', 'Karen/David'.

- Spell the person's name correctly. Add their name to your dictionary if you are going to email the person often, especially if the name has accents/unusual spelling.

- Use a greeting that reflects the existing level of the relationship. For example, when emailing a new prospect, it will usually be a formal 'Dear John', 'Dear Mr Smith'. As you get to know each other, greetings may become less formal – 'Hi John', but only if the dialogue suggests this will be well received – i.e. you have spoken or the recipient has emailed you and used a less formal salutation.

- When responding to email containing a greeting, mirror the initial salutation.

- Add a greeting even when replying to an email which has no greeting.

Don't

- Use nicknames and abbreviations unless the other person has used them.

 recap

Greetings in email are the handshakes of electronic communication.

● Always start your email with a salutation which reflects current standing and formality of the relationship.

● Vary the greeting as you get to know the recipient better and the relationship builds.

● When responding to an email for the first time, mirror the way the sender addressed you. If they did not include a greeting, start your reply with their name.

CHAPTER 13

Pen your message in plain language

Proper punctuation is both the sign and cause of clear thinking.

Lynne Truss

I n the days of traditional work and fixed office routines, how you dressed was all important. Today, in the age of flexible working and mobile communication, the way you write your email has taken over as the 'textual dress code' of the twenty-first century. This chapter covers the fourth element of crafting excellent emails and includes:

- Guidelines on writing the content/body to convey the right message, right first time to reduce the rounds of email ping-pong.
- Bridging the gender gap to improve relationships.
- Guidelines on fonts to use for email that can be read regardless of device and visual impairment.
- Timesaving software functions to help you write an email, such as text templates.

Why should an email be as perfect as a letter?

In addition to the fact that email creates a picture of you in the mind of the reader, there are two other reasons why well crafted content is critical:

1 Professional business brand and personal images can take years, if not generations, to build, yet can be destroyed in a nanosecond by a sloppy, ill-thought-out email. Take the one sent at 14.45 on 9 September from Jo Moore (a civil servant) to Stephen Byers, the then Transport Minister. She said that 'Today (9/11) would be a good time to "bury" some controversial stories.' Both their personal reputations were damaged and Ms Moore was moved sideways. Dealing with email media disasters like these costs time and often money as a damage limitation campaign must be launched. For more email disasters, see www.brilliant-email.com.

2 Emails can be used as legal evidence in court. This aspect of email is dealt with in Chapter 17.

The 'Three Cs' of a good email

If you can't explain it simply, you don't understand it well enough.
: Albert Einstein

How often have you lost time reading and re-reading an email but still could not understand what it is saying, let alone what is being asked of you? Often this confusion of meaning is caused by one-word responses, as in this example:

---

brilliant example

Frank is responding to a revised quotation sent by Clare.

To: Clare Mann

From: Frank Brown

Subject: Budget for project management workshop

Hi Clare

OK.

Regards Frank

What does OK mean? 'OK, Frank has accepted Clare's quotation'; 'OK, Frank will discuss it with his manager'? Or simply, 'OK thanks, Clare, I will get back to you'?

Then there are those long, densely packed emails that often spread to at least three quarters of a page. In my own case, both these types of emails are usually parked in a pending folder until I find time to try to sort out just what is happening (usually by phone).

Emails that are easy to comprehend generally follow the 'Three Cs' rule. They are:

- **Concise** – tell you up-front the essential information you need to make a decision.
- **Crisp** – use simple words conveying exactly what is intended and make sense.
- **Clear** – are well laid out to make them easy to read (on any size screen).

Making emails easy to read

Look at the emails you have received today and pick one which was quick and easy to read and one which was hard. Compare them and pick out the features which made them easy versus hard. Use the template in Table 13.1.

Table 13.1

Easy to read – aspects	Hard to read – aspects

How well does your list compare with the 'Three Cs' rules?

The 'Three C's' of writing emails will help you gain and maintain the reader's attention and respect. They are a way of ensuring an email is easy to read, regardless of the device being used, any visual impairment and command of the English language. In today's global business world it is also critical to make sure your message can be understood by those whose mother tongue may not be English. Words can often be easily misinterpreted and cause problems. Moreover, and perhaps not surprisingly, there are often gaps between the way men and women word and interpret emails.

To help you bridge these gaps and improve the probability of conveying the right message first time, in the following section we provide guidelines on:

● wording
● layout
● fonts and colour
● bridging the gender gap.

These will help you apply the 'Three Cs' and be an even more effective email communicator.

Wording

What happens when it (punctuation) isn't used. Well if punctuation is the stitching of language, language comes apart, and obviously all the buttons fall off. If punctuation provides the traffic signals, words bang into each other and everyone ends up in Minehead.
                                        Lynne Truss from *Eats Shoots and Leaves*

Email's lack of surrounding contextual information means 'KISS' in all its forms for email is vital – Keep It Short and Simple. Keep It Simple, Stupid. Keep it Simple and Straightforward.

Based on my work with clients and some of the best emails I

have received, here are some guidelines about wording of emails to help you save time.

⭐ brilliant dos and don'ts

[handwritten margin note: does this exist in googlemail ?]

Do

- Write in grammatically correct English sentences.
- Punctuate correctly (for example, distinguish between 'its' and 'it's').
- Use words that most people will understand.
- Use industry-specific terminology as appropriate.
- Spell check before sending but be careful that the meanings of words are not changed (for example, 'inconvenience' to 'incontinence', 'public' to 'pubic').
- Add unusual words to the dictionary to ensure they are correctly spelt in future.
- Add accents as appropriate.

Don't use

- Jargon and slang, as both can easily be misunderstood.
- Text-speak and emoticons.
- Words that might be regarded as racist, defamatory and discriminatory.
- Copyright material, unless you have permission.

One client has a handbook of preferred phrases and words, which includes those to be avoided as they may be problematic if used in a court of law.

Layout

After picking the right words, how you lay them out is the next most important aspect of a good email. Have you ever wondered why some emails look like alphabet spaghetti when you open them? Fancy formatting and fonts are often lost in transmission, especially if the sender and recipient are using different email software systems. Also, if one party is using a handheld email device, much of the formatting can be lost.

brilliant tip

Break up and space out the content of an email.

Save time as a sender and help preserve the impact of your content by minimising the time spent formatting emails (as in italics, fancy bullet points and colour). Instead, maximise the use of white space between different points.

Here are seven simple ways to enhance your message by adding visual impact. This will create synergy with the words you have used rather than distract from them. After all, there is not much point in spending time carefully phrasing the content if the finished article is hard to read, either because the original layout was poor or it has been lost in transmission.

create synergy with the words you have used

Top seven tips for laying out an email to enhance the impact of the words

1 Use the top-down newspaper approach – start with the headline and then add any supporting information.

2 Structure the content just as you would a letter.

3 Number and separate each key point/section with white space (i.e. a blank line).

4 Use plain text rather than HTML and rich text, as not all email software translates and renders HTML properly.

5 Avoid capitals (they look like you are shouting) and italics (they are hard to read).

6 Limit the content to half a page (any more and it suggests you need a properly formatted document sent as an attachment).

7 Keep to one topic per email – don't slip in an extra topic at the end of the email. This is highly likely to be missed.

Most email software allows you to select what format you use for your emails. In Outlook go to 'Tools/Options' and select the 'Mail Format' tab (Figure 13.1). Then select 'Plain text' from the 'Message format' drop down menu.

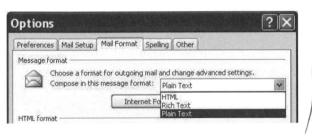

Figure 13.1 Setting the default format to plain text

Fonts and colour

Many organisations have set standards based on their branding. For those who have the choice and want some guidelines on how to make your email look professional and legible on most devices and to most people, here are some suggestions. Use:

- sans serif fonts, which are easy to read onscreen, such as Arial, Verdana or Courier
- font size of between 10 and 12pt
- black or blue for the text. They are generally regarded as the easiest colours to read and are neutral in the image they create

- consistent colour and font throughout, including the signature block.

The options above also reduce the email's size, hence storage space, and the amount of paper and toner consumed if your email needs printing – all of which helps the green economy.

Catering for visual impairment

Through my *Times* Crème 'PC Stress Busters' column, I acquired an email penfriend, the late Bishop Richard Hare, whose sight was failing him. He wrote the most eloquent and informative emails. We emailed for nearly five years about everything from families to politics. I used a large font – minimum 16pt to make it easy for him to read. Richard was very IT-literate and knew how to enlarge the font if I forgot. Others may not be so IT capable.

If you are emailing someone who is visually impaired, here are four ways to help them. These are based on emailing Richard and working with Wessex Disability and guidance from their CEO Nikki Haswell.

1   Never assume what font or format the visually impaired recipient will need: ask each one because there are a great number of different kinds of visual impairment that affects what they can see.

2   If you are sending documents as attachments, check in which format to send it. This is because screen reader software does not always work properly (for example) with a pdf but does with Word.

3   Keep messages concise and to the point. It takes longer for a screen reader to read out the text of a message than it would for a sighted person to scan an email, and reading magnified text is also slower.

4   Remember that highlighting words in a different colour
or bold will not work for someone using screen reader
software.

Bridging the gender gap

Is there a noticeable difference between the way men and
women use email?

Take an email from a male and a female colleague and compare
using the template below.

Table 13.2 Differences in men and women's email

Criterion	Male colleague's email	Female colleague's email
Greeting		
Tone		
Focus		
Sign-off		
Others		

Did it strike you that there were differences? How well do these
variations mirror the differences between how your male and
female colleagues behave and communicate in general?

Not surprisingly, research, including my own, has shown that the
differences between how men and women operate in business
(and socially) carries over into how they communicate. For an
in-depth review see *Gender and Communication at Work* edited by
Mary Barrett and Marilyn Davidson. Drawing on earlier work
in *Managing in the Email Office* by Monica Seeley and Gerard
Hargreaves, here is a summary of some of the common difference in email communications.

Table 13.3 Summary of common differences in emails

Criterion	Men and email	Women and email
Deleting	Often	Hoarders, keeping too much 'just in case'
Subject line	Limited	More accurate
Salutation	Often none	Nearly always included
Tone	Terse	Flowery
Content	Shorter, crisper and to the point	Rambling and often flowery
Gossip	Often – the main culprits of email media disasters	Rarely
Imagery	Rarely included, but occasional text-speak emoticons	Often use stationery and smileys
Sign-off	Professional, bland but can be terse	Flowery, often use colour and fancy fonts

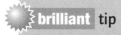

Do you recognise yourself?

brilliant tip

To benchmark whether your emails are from Mars or Venus go to www.brilliant-email.com and use the 'Email Clarity' checklist.

Here are the top five tips to bridge the gender gap and make sure you continue to convey the 'right message right first time'.

Table 13.4 Bridge the gender gap

Men should	Women should
Vary opening and closing to reflect the status quo and level of the business relationship	Vary opening and closing to reflect the status quo and level of the business relationship
Omit the text-speak	Use a plain black font throughout and forget the stationery and smileys
Add feelings	Shorten emails and focus on the task in hand
Stop gossiping online about your sex life	Hit 'Delete' more often

 example

One female client who felt she had quite an abrupt manner often sent her emails to a colleague to check for tone and textual imagery before sending them to the client. She felt this significantly improved how her emails were received and hence their impact on the business relationship.

Software functions to help you save time

Do you ever need to re-send the same email content to different people at different times? For example, when responding to job applicants, confirming arrangements for a meeting, thanking people for a contribution to an article/book?

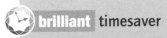 timesaver

Creating templates of re-usable text is a great timesaver when you need to send a similar email to multiple people at different times.

There are a number of ways to create templates of text:

- Copy and paste the text from a previous email.
- Use the signature block in Outlook 2003 and Entourage.
- Quick Parts in Outlook 2007.

 brilliant recap ~~*STAFF HANDBOOK*~~

- Adopt the 'Three Cs' rules for writing – Concise, Crisp and Clear.
- Structure the content and separate out key information.
- Before hitting 'Send', check that your emails are all 'PEARLS', crafted to save time and contribute positively to the business relationship:

  P **PROPERLY** laid out

  E Written in plain grammatically correct **ENGLISH**

  A Have an **ACCURATE** subject line

  R **RELATE** to business

  L **LESS** than half a screen in length

  S About a **SINGLE** topic

- Use a plain black 10 or 12pt font consistently throughout the email.
- Increase the font size only when sending to those who are visually impaired.
- Develop a style guide for your business if one doesn't already exist.
- Use software functions to help save you time.

CHAPTER 14

Saying goodbye professionally

What was cold soon warms, and warmth soon cools.

Heraclitus

How you say 'goodbye' is just as important as how you say 'hello'. A lackadaisical sign-off can sabotage all your hard work crafting the content of your email. This chapter covers closing an email, the last element of crafting an excellent email:

● Closing sign-off

● Signature block

● Company information and disclaimers

---

brilliant example

What picture do you instantly form of Luke and Lucinda from their sign-offs as shown below?

1. Cheers, Luke

2. Lucinda X

Now assume you have exchanged several rounds of email and you wish to speak to Luke or Lucinda. Can you quickly find their contact details? With luck they are at the end of their initial email. Can you be bothered to trawl back? No. So you continue the email dialogue, but with your image of Luke and Lucinda tarnished by their lack of an adequate signature.

Signing off to keep communications flowing

Put as much thought into how to sign off an email as you did into the greeting and the content. See the sign-off as the cufflinks/jewellery you would choose to supplement your overall attire. Here are some tips for creating sign-offs which will add the finishing touches to your email dress code:

- Always add a sign-off phrase before your name. Those which convey a professional image include: 'Kind regards', 'Regards', 'Yours', 'Best wishes', 'Many thanks', 'Thanks'.
- Avoid phrases like 'Cheers', 'Best' and 'Bestest', which often create a casual, laidback image.
- Only use text-speak when you know the person really well and take care even then. Just because the other person uses text-speak, that doesn't mean you have to drop your email dress code.

Signature blocks

My surveys have found that when an email exchange is going nowhere, the lack of contact details after your sign-off is probably the major barrier to picking up the phone. Ask yourself, which would you rather do? Send a quick email or wade through pages on the intranet to find a phone number?

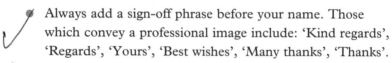

brilliant tip

Always include at least your telephone number at the end of every email exchange (both internal and external).

What contact information you include in your signature block may well be dictated by your business email policy and/or communications policy. Nonetheless, a hotly debated topic is how much information and whether or not to include straplines and logos in signature blocks. The choice seems to be the 'full monty' versus a minimal approach.

- Full contact details versus minimal essential information.
- Corporate logo, special awards and event logos versus no images.
- Straplines and value statements versus nothing.
- Layout – sequentially down the page versus across the page.

Minimal is best as it takes up less paper and storage. Email is not the place to be creating graphic brand images other than through the presentation of the email's message (from greeting to sign-off). Furthermore, icons that usually appear as JPEG attachments increase the risk of the email being trapped as spam, because JPEG-type attachments can harbour viruses.

minimal is best

Here is an example of the minimalist approach, which tells you all you need to know about the sender (Robert) and how to contact him.

 **brilliant example** *Consider*

Robert Boxer| Managing Editor| Super Books Ltd| Tel: +44 (1) 0207 123 4567| www.superbooks.com| Follow us on Twitter at http://twitter.com/superbooks

In workshops and discussions, fancy signature blocks are often listed among the top ten things which annoy people. The following tips will help to add that final professional touch to your email.

☆ brilliant dos and don'ts

Do

- Include:

    a. Your name in full

    b   Position/Job title

    c. Full company name

    d. Telephone number in international format (and mobile number if appropriate)

    e. Web address

    f. Social networking details (Twitter and LinkedIn, etc.)

- Spread it across the page rather than down.

- Use the same font style and colour as the body of your email, but reduce the font size slightly (for example, by one or two points).

Don't

- Include:

    a. Corporate logos and awards (for example, Publishers of the Year)

    b. Value statements

    c. Full postal address – the recipient can ask if it's needed

    d. Fax number – unless fax plays an important part in your business

    e. Environmental messages (for example, 'Don't print this email unless necessary')

- Change font style and colour from the one used in the body of the email and/or increase the font size.

Signature blocks adhering to these guidelines means that everyone uses fewer resources (paper, toner, server space etc.). Images of logos can add up to 50KB to each email. This is like adding extra weight when posting a letter so that the letter then costs 50p more to post. Emails with logos take up more space and need more bandwidth to transmit.

Use your email software to save time with the sign-off and signature block

Most software has a function which allows you to add automatically your sign-off and signature block to all new emails and replies. In Outlook, go to the 'Tools/Options/Mail Format' tab and click on 'Signatures'.

Most software allows you to have several templates between which you can toggle. Multiple templates are a great timesaver when you need to vary your signature – for example, for internal and external email, or to include a seasons greeting at New Year.

A typical internal sign-off might simply be: 'Kind regards, Robert Boxer, Ext 789'. For external emails Robert could insert his minimal one shown earlier on page 183.

Company information and disclaimers

These are the last two elements of a brilliant email. Do you need them? Yes and no. This is a complex area and you should consult a lawyer who understands e-commerce law.

Company information

If you are a limited company, you must include company registration number, place of registration and registered office address. Otherwise you will be in breach of the 1 January 2007 amendment to the Companies Act 1985. They are not required for sole traders and standard partnerships.

Disclaimers

These have never been tested in a court of law. Nonetheless, the advice is to add a short disclaimer as it may help limit damages against your company. The emphasis is on the words 'short' and 'may'. Disclaimers should cover confidentiality and any email monitoring processes (such as for content and viruses). Generally, in large businesses these are automatically appended by your email server. For smaller organisations you should consult with both your email provider and a reliable legal adviser.

 brilliant recap

- Use phrases that convey a professional image such as 'Kind regards' and 'Thank you'.

- Avoid phrases that may be perceived as casual and lackadaisical, like 'Cheers'.

- On every email exchange, always include your phone number as a minimum. For external emails, make sure it's in international format.

- For external emails, keep the signature block short and simple. Include basic information about your role, telephone contact details, website and social networking details as appropriate.

- Forget all those logos, marketing slogans and environmentally friendly straplines. They just distract and bulk up your email unnecessarily.

- Save yourself time by using your email software to add automatically your personal sign-off and contact details to both new emails and replies.

- For limited companies, make sure you include your key company details.

- Add a short disclaimer on confidentiality and monitoring, which may limit any liability in a court case.

Managing attachments for extra efficiency

'Too often I find the volume of paper expands to fill the available briefcases.'

Jerry Brown

Attachments are the pariahs of mailbox and business storage space. They can also be the source of accidentally leaking confidential data and opening the door to viruses. Not surprisingly, attachments carry their own health warnings.

Part 4 provides ways to save time by smartly managing your use of attachments, both as sender and as recipient.

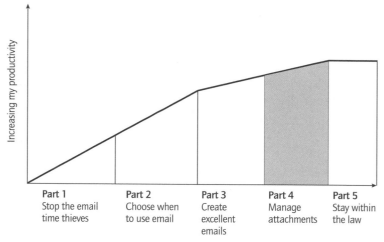

Five steps to improving my productivity – managing attachments

How many times have you received that annoying and at times distressing message saying 'You are now over your mailbox limit'? If you are too far over, you may not be able to send or receive any more emails. This means that you have to stop and immediately take steps to reduce your mailbox: depending on your system, you may find yourself locked out of your mailbox for a few hours.

Have you ever inadvertently sent a file which reveals all the internal comments on a document? This might be highly sensitive data which should never have been seen by anyone outside the business. In 2006 Google accidentally revealed confidential financial data because comments (written as reminders to the presenter) were left in a slide presentation when it was later distributed. The revelation caused the shares to slip by 2 per cent.

Do you ever send emails with attachments only to find that the recipient has not received them because they are too large? This can entail losing valuable time as you try to sort out the matter, perhaps by shrinking the size of the attachment.

The blunt way that has been developed to manage the burden imposed by the growing volume and size of attachments is through the imposition of mailbox limits and restrictions on attachment sizes and content. They are not unlike highway speed cameras – they act as a powerful deterrent and ignoring them can be very costly. However, they do not really address the fundamental underlying problem of poor email management.

Taking personal control of how you handle attachments is a far more effective way to save time and increase your productivity rather than relying on the limits of the system.

CHAPTER 15

Sending attachments – smart behaviour

An employee who earns $60,000 a year and wastes five minutes a day (dealing with version control, file formats and other document related problems) costs an organisation $635 per year in lost productivity.

Osterman Research, 2009

How much are you costing yourself and your business by behaving thoughtlessly with attachments? Email seduces us into circulating huge volumes of attachments, very few of which are really needed by the recipient, as shown by the results of our research in Figure 15.1.

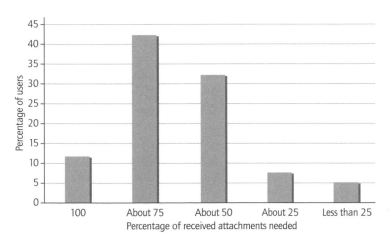

Figure 15.1 Volume of unnecessary attachments

This chapter covers patrolling your use of attachments as a sender to:

- improve the chance of your email being well received by the recipient
- increase security and confidentiality
- raise the probability of everyone working with the correct version of the file (spreadsheet, document, etc).

Email limits – a necessary evil?

There are several reasons why organisations impose restrictions on attachment sizes.

1 Attachments use valuable bandwidth as they are transmitted (sent/received). To preserve your email system's reliability (especially speed and stability), most businesses need to restrict the size of attachments that can be transmitted during normal working hours: this is usually between 5 and 20 MB. Emails over the limit are held for sending/delivery until after normal working hours.

2 Network bandwidth and speed is directly proportional to cost.

3 Carbon footprints are directly related to mailbox sizes, because more bandwidth and storage consumes more energy.

Is there scope to save time in the way I handle attachments as a sender?

Attachment dumping is the fastest way to annoy people and waste everyone's time. These are the top seven attachment time thieves for recipients, all of which are caused by the sender:

1 Missing attachments.

2 Large attachments that do not reach the recipient on time.

3   Sending multiple attachments in a single email.

4   Not working with the most current version of the file.

5   Not saving attachments so they can be found quickly and easily.

6   Sending/receiving attachments containing hidden confidential metadata (changes made by the originator such as revisions, by whom and when).

7   Sending/receiving attachments containing viruses and malware.

Improving how you manage attachments both as a sender and as a recipient will help you and others recoup further time from the email thieves.

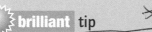

brilliant tip

Always attach your file first, then write your email. This reduces the likelihood of another round of email ping-pong to resolve the missing attachment dilemma.

Keeping attachment sizes within limits

Here are four simple ways to check and reduce the size of the attachments you send to ensure you stay within the limit for transmission during working hours.

1   Find out about both your own and the recipient's limit for transmitting emails during the working day.

2   Check the file size either from the folder list (in Explorer) or right-click on the file itself. Microsoft (PC) users should pick 'Properties' from the drop-down menu; Apple users should pick 'Get Info'.

3   Compress (zip) large attachments (over 5 MB) using proprietary software like WinZip and Stuffit.

4   If the compressed file is still large, either split the contents and send the files in separate emails or compress the original file. For example, reduce the resolution of images.

The actions outlined above increase the likelihood of your email being delivered on time and promote a more professional image by sparing you the embarrassing 'Where is it?' email chain/phone call.

Efficient ways to send multiple attachments

Often several files need to be attached to single emails (for example, for board meetings, sales presentations, budget and personnel reviews). The main challenge facing recipients of multiple attachments are:

● being sure that they have them all

● the reading order

● which attachment, if any, specifically requires their attention.

Time is then squandered by email dialogues while recipients clarify what has been sent and what is required of them.

> ☀ **brilliant** tip
>
> Include a 'Read me first' file that lists how many files are attached and their reading order.

Five more tips to make friends not enemies and impress recipients when sending multiple attachments are:

1   Limit the total number in a single email to seven.

2   Zip the files into one main file (again using proprietary software such as WinZip and Stuffit).

3   Label each file with an intelligent and self-explanatory name.

4   Where there are multiple recipients, draw individuals' attention to files (and sections) that require their specific scrutiny.

5   If some recipients only need to see certain pages tell them which ones.

These tips raise the likelihood of everyone reading the files properly, being better briefed and generally able to work more productively. You also reduce the carbon footprint of attachments: as there is nothing more annoying and wasteful than printing a large document only to find you needed only one page. Plus patrolling your use of attachments continues to enhance your email dress code.

> enhance your email dress code

Sharing to reduce the volume of unnecessary attachments and data leakage

The uncontrolled circulation of attachments gives rise to a number of challenges:

● Files become out of date almost as soon as they are sent: a revised version has to then be sent immediately after. This seems to happen often with meeting papers and budgets.

● Everyone keeps their own copy (copies).

● People work from different versions of the file.

● There is a high risk of breach of compliance, because attachments are sometimes retained which by law should be deleted. (For example, under the Data Protection Act personal data such as CVs should be deleted once they are no longer relevant.)

● Copies are printed 'just in case'.

DROP BOX

brilliant tip

Put files in a shared area and send a link to it, rather than the actual file.

File sharing (either through the network or collaborative tools like Notes or Microsoft SharePoint) substantially reduces the unnecessary drain on resources, from your personal time to your server space and carbon footprint. It also increases ·the probability of everyone working from the correct file version and minimises the risk of a breach of compliance and security as you can control access to the file.

Securing the content from being distorted

While attachments are not quite as vulnerable as the body of an email, they are not tamper-proof. Furthermore, the contents can still reveal hidden confidential information in the form of metadata (track changes, number of revisions, etc.). Many organisations have found themselves put at significant financial and reputational risk through employees leaving metadata in files, as outlined in the introduction to this part.

---

brilliant example

The 'Dodgy Dossier' incident (2002) was created through the metadata left in the UK government files. Analysis of the metadata revealed that files had been plagiarised from other non-government sources (a postgraduate thesis) and that the edits had been made to make the case for Iraq's ability to produce nuclear weapons.

✖ brilliant dos and don'ts

Do

- Clean up attachments before sending them – for example, remove track changes, comments and hidden columns.

- Use a function like the 'Inspector' in Word 2007 or a specialist product like Workshare™ and ConfidentSend™. *ALWAYS*

- Unless you are expecting the recipient to work on them, convert and send the file as a pdf.

- Password-protect (or encrypt) the files if they contain highly sensitive and confidential information.

- Send an original hand copy if you have any concerns that the recipient might alter an electronic version and then present their version as the authentic one.

Don't

- Assume that because you have sent the document as a pdf, the recipient cannot change the contents. Using Acrobat Professional, any pdf file can be opened and changed. (Sadly, even if you encrypt the pdf, there is software which lets the recipient decrypt it and tamper with it.)

For more information on this subject see 'A Guide to Document Comparison and Security for Corporate Legal' from Osterman Research – www.ostermanresearch.com.

Cleaning up attachments not only improves productivity but also protects your reputation and minimises the risk of leaking confidential information.

Attachments and handheld email devices

Attachments can present a problem to those accessing their emails on a handheld email device such as a BlackBerry or iPhone, as older models often do not download and display attachments satisfactorily. This is changing. Nonetheless, it is always worth checking first with the recipient.

brilliant tip

If the recipient is working on a handheld email device, paste just the critical part/executive summary of the attachment into the body of the email.

Microsoft Office 2007 lets you send the file you are working on directly from within the application without opening the email application. Go to the 'Office' button and pick 'Send'. This will open up your email software and you can either attach or insert the file automatically.

brilliant recap

Patrolling your use of attachments as a sender and recipient will help you reclaim further time from email time thieves, reduce your carbon footprint and further enhance your email dress code.

● Send a link rather than the actual file wherever possible.

● When sending more than five files in one email, attach a 'Read me first' note telling the recipient how many files to expect, what they are about and the reading order. Draw to their attention to sections/pages that require their specific attention.

● Viewing attachments on handheld email devices can be difficult. Copy and paste key information into the body of the email.

● Clean attachments before sending to remove any potentially damaging metadata.

● Protect and secure the contents of attachments which are sensitive, confidential and may be regarded as legally binding.

CHAPTER 16

Receiving attachments – saving time

A 1 MB file is equivalent to a 500-page book. 100 MB is about 2.4 metres (2.8 yards) of text.

Attachments, rather than the number of emails, are the main cause of exceeding your mailbox limit. Your mailbox size comprises the sum of all the emails in your 'Received', 'Sent' and 'Deleted' folders. The quickest way to downsize your mailbox is therefore clearly to remove and delete all large attachments. However, it's quite common to forget to empty the 'Deleted' folder. Until you empty the 'Deleted' folder, all those large email attachments remain in your mailbox.

After deleting attachments, the other significant email time thief is subsequently finding the file. Attachments can also be virus carriers. This chapter covers patrolling your use of attachments as a recipient in order to:

attachments can also be virus carriers

- keep within mailbox limits
- be able to find files quickly
- reduce the risk of handling an infected file.

Saving and finding attachments more speedily and staying within limits

Many people simply leave all the attachments with the original email (sent and received). Their justification is that this is the easiest way subsequently to find them. This is debatable and has the key disadvantage that it will contribute towards your mailbox size. Furthermore, what happens if the email system goes down (as discussed in Chapter 6)?

brilliant tip

Save attachments in your personal area on the main network. If working remotely with limited network connectivity, save them to your laptop's hard drive.

Here are five further tips to help you to find stored attachments quickly and easily and keep your mailbox within limits:

1 Once you have saved the attachment, remove it from the email. Right-click on the file and choose 'Remove'.

2 Remove unnecessary attachments from emails you forward (as above).

3 Re-name the file(s) as necessary.

4 If you are working off-site, make sure you back up your laptop regularly.

5 Remove all attachments that you send – they too will weigh down your mailbox and as you are the sender you should have the original file!

Using either the desktop search function, which comes with your PC (or Mac), or an application like Google Desktop Search, you should be able to find the file within a few seconds.

Handling attachments that may be infected

Attachments are harbingers of viruses and malware (the stuff which can wreak havoc with your computer).

brilliant tip

Never open suspicious and/or unexpected attachments, especially those which have file extensions such as '.exe', '.bat', '.dll' and '.cmd'.

These days suspicious attachments are generally detected immediately by anti-virus software (either on your PC or from your email host). If you do receive a suspicious attachment, here are four ways to prevent them from damaging your computer and/or network.

1 Never open the attachment until you have checked with the sender what it contains.

2 If it's legitimate, re-scan it with your own anti-virus software (it still may have picked up a virus *en route* to you). If it still shows signs of being infected, ask the sender to re-send a clean copy.

3 Delete it straightaway if it's not legitimate.

4 Follow your business/email supplier's guidelines for handling suspect attachments.

This will save you time and money by limiting (even negating) the need to disinfect your computer and/or network. The subject of viruses and malware is dealt with in more detail in Chapter 18.

Googlemail limits? (handwritten)

Timesaving software functions

Staying well within your mailbox limits ensures that if on a busy day you receive several large attachments you will still be able to send and receive emails. Most email systems allow some flexibility but if you exceed a certain limit, your mailbox will be instantly frozen. Even if you immediately downsize, it may take the mail server a few hours to register this and reactivate your mailbox.

Software like Outlook, Notes, GroupWise and Entourage provide a number of functions to let you check your mailbox size.

brilliant tip

Keep within 75 per cent of your allowed mailbox limit.

Keeping a check on your mailbox size in Outlook

Here are three key software functions to help you check your mailbox size and look for large attachments:

1 Size field – make sure this is visible on all folders.

2 Mailbox size – accessed in Outlook via 'Mailbox Cleanup'.

3 Search folders – specific to Outlook 2007 and upwards. 'Large Mail' gives a virtual view of your mailbox by size.

 **recap**

● Managing the attachments in your mailbox as a recipient helps you reclaim further time from email time thieves and reduce your carbon footprint.

● Check your mailbox limit and keep to within 75 per cent of your allowance.

● Save attachments you receive with other files to which they relate (for example, client/project file) and then remove them from the email itself.

● When working remotely, if you think you may have limited network connection, make sure you have the attachments saved to your laptop hard drive.

● Never open suspicious attachments. Delete them and ask for them to be re-sent if they are from legitimate senders.

PART 5

Stay the right side of the law

'Nearly half (48 per cent) of e-disclosure cases cost £500,000 or more, with over a quarter (26 per cent) costing more than £1 million.'

KPMG survey 'e-Disclosure: The 21st Century Legal Challenge'

This part of the book provides a brief overview of:

● key legislation governing email, ways to limit your personal liability and avoid starring in an email-generated media scandal and tribunal

● top tips to protect yourself from cyber-crime and the costs relating to disinfecting your computer and network.

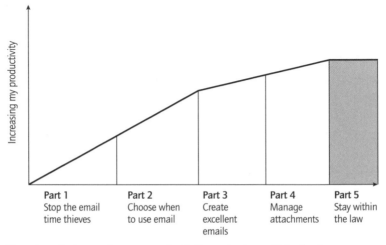

Part 1	Part 2	Part 3	Part 4	Part 5
Stop the email time thieves	Choose when to use email	Create excellent emails	Manage attachments	Stay within the law

Five steps to improving my productivity – staying within the law

E-disclosure is the term applied to the use of digital documents (including emails) as evidence in a trial. The laws relating to email are many and complex. Some have been touched upon in Chapter 14 (for example, the Companies Act).

It is easy to leak company confidential data. Pricewaterhouse-Coopers (PwC) 'Information Security Breaches Survey' in 2010 found that 83 to 92 per cent of business had suffered some form of security breach. The cost of a breach of compliance and security can be expensive. PwC estimated it ranged from £28,000 for a small company (less than 50 staff) to half a million for a large business (more than 500 staff). Not all incidents were email-induced, but email is nonetheless a major source of cyber-crime in terms of spreading viruses, malware (software which harms your PC) and phishing attacks (luring you to bogus websites to disclose details of a web account, generally financial). The PwC survey revealed that security breaches had trebled in the last two years and are rising.

The 2007 KPMG Forensic survey, 'e-Disclosure: The 21st Century Legal Challenge' alarmingly found that many high court judges and senior court officials are ill equipped to deal with e-evidence.

There is therefore scope to be even more productive both as an individual and a business, if you take measures to stay on the right side of the law and protect yourself (and your business) from cyber-crime. This is the last step in the personal journey to squeeze those extra few efficiency gains from using email effectively.

CHAPTER 17

Email as evidence

The only thing we know about the future is that it is going to be different.

Peter Drucker

The laws that relate to the use of email as evidence are not only complicated but also depend on the sector in which you work (public or private) and where your business is located. For example, in the UK public sector, the Freedom of Information Act plays an important role. In the USA, many businesses and public bodies are regulated by the Sarbanes-Oxley Act.

This chapter provides a brief overview of:

- the top five acts that apply to most UK email users
- key implications for your use of email
- tips to stay the right side of the law
- sources of more detailed information on email and the law.

The KPMG survey 'e-Disclosure: The 21st Century Legal Challenge' found that 95 per cent of respondents regarded business email as an important source of digital evidence. The free-flow nature of email can make it hard to control who sees what and hence how to reduce the risk of breaches of security and compliance.

From my discussions with clients, the primary concerns for most business email users are:

- How to manage data leakage and breach of copyright through forwarded emails.
- How to ensure emails are properly stored (in case they are needed as evidence).
- The best way to ensure all concerned understand and comply with the law?

STAFF HANDBOOK

brilliant tip

Never put anything in an email that you would not be able to defend in a court of law.

Top five acts regulating the use of email in the UK

The key UK acts regulating most business (and indeed non-business) use of email are outlined in this section, along with their key implications and dos and don'ts.

Data Protection Act 1988

This protects your right to protect personal data about yourself; this includes your email address. It also covers, for example, personal information contained in your CV when applying for a job, information relating to sick leave, and a mortgage application. In 2010, fines of up to £500,000 were introduced by the Information Commissioner for breaches of security and confidentiality.

check Bev

The key implication is that you must ensure you destroy emails which contain private information once the incident to which they relate is closed, unless it is needed for a valid reason. When emailing personal data check that your email is secure.

Computer Misuse Usage Act 1990

This covers the unauthorised access and use of a computer with the intent to commit a crime.

The key implication is that you must not circulate emails which could be deemed to be a breach of any of the laws of the land. For example, under the Equal Opportunities Commission 2006 guidelines, lewd, racist or pornographic emails can now be regarded as evidence of sexual harassment by a person, even if that person has not seen them but knows of their existence.

Regulation Investigatory Power Act 2000

This allows public bodies to intercept and monitor data flows if their use is suspected to cause a major national security breach, disorder (strike), anti-competitive practices, etc. For example, in 2007 Tesco and Asda were ordered to hand over millions of emails in an anti-competitive investigation.

However, the Human Rights Act 1998 and European Convention on Human Rights can also protect you if you feel the monitoring is unjustified. This was demonstrated by the case of Lynette Copland who successfully took the UK government to court after Carmarthenshire College monitored her internet usage and telephone calls. She won €3,000 plus damages.

The key implication is that you should be aware that your computer could be seized by the police and your emails used as evidence. However, make sure you have a watertight case for monitoring individuals and tell them if doing so.

Human Rights Act 1998

This protects your right to enjoy a working environment which does not breach and violate your privacy and does not subject you to abuse and discrimination.

The key implication is that emails which are considered a breach of your human rights can be used as evidence, even if you have not seen them but know that they exist.

Freedom of Information Act 2000 (FOIA)

Under this act, anyone is entitled to request to see information from a public body (local council, police health authority, etc.) on a subject which interests them. The 2009 MPs' expenses scandal was mainly sparked by FOI requests. Clever use of the FOI Act can enable you to gain competitive information during a public sector tendering exercise.

The key implication is that emails can and often are provided as evidence. On the one hand, you must retain emails if required to provide them, and on the other you must be able to demonstrate you have destroyed emails which contain data which should not be retained.

How can I stay within the law?

Many of the first-tier best practices to enable you to stay the right side of the law have been spelt out in Parts 2 to 4. Here is a synthesis of the essential top-level tips to help you reduce the risks of email evidence being used against you and your business.

 **dos and don'ts**

Do

- Review your email before sending to ensure that it does not contain any information which might cause embarrassment to you or your business.

- Keep to facts rather than opinions. When you do include the latter, preface by attributing it to yourself rather than your business (for example, 'In my personal opinion …').

- When emailing personal information take care that your email is secure.

- Check that you are sending your email to the right person (i.e. the right John Smith).

- When forwarding an email, be certain that you are not sending copyright protected information without the original sender's permission.

- If you are in international business check what laws regulate your use of email, especially if you are registered in the USA.

- When sending emails which contain highly sensitive competitive information to a public body, add a line which limits content from being disclosed without your knowledge in an FOIA enquiry.

- Make sure key emails are properly archived and can be easily searched and retrieved if necessary.

Don't

- Include content in an email that you could not defend in court.

- Include any material that might be regarded as racist, abusive, defamatory, pornographic, etc.

- Send jokes – these can be misinterpreted and could be regarded as a contravention of the Human Rights Act.

- Forward emails to non-business email addresses without consent from your business as this can cause a security breach and data leakage.

- Retain emails containing personal information for longer than necessary.

- Attempt to circumvent your business's Acceptable Usage Policy (AUP) and especially the limits of transmission of attachments (see below for more on this).

Acceptable usage policy (AUP)

One of the basic ways to ensure everyone is properly informed about the behaviour deemed acceptable to your specific business is to have an internal business specific Acceptable Usage Policy (AUP).

brilliant tip

Benchmark your AUP at www.brilliant-email.com.

It is not sufficient to simply write the policy. You also need to ensure that:

- staff are fully aware and have formally accepted your business's Acceptable Usage Policy (AUP).
- it is kept up to date to reflect changes in technology and legislation.

Failure to ensure that everyone is aware of and signed up to the policy can be costly. In 2004 Royal Bank of Scotland lost a case of unfair dismissal against an employee for sending pornographic emails. The employee won because she demonstrated she had not been fully aware of the bank's process for grading emails as offensive.

Acceptance and awareness can be achieved through distributing the policy, having employees sign to indicate formal acceptance, providing prompts each time people log on to their computer, and providing a comprehensive education policy.

Useful sources of further information

Understanding the law as applied to email is a minefield. Five excellent sources of further information are:

1   www.ico.gov.uk – the UK Information Commissioners Office

2   www.is4profit.com – a free information website for small businesses

3   www.mimecast.com – for white papers

4   www.sophos.com – for white papers

5. www.out-law.com – for case histories.

🔆 **brilliant** recap

Emails are frequently used as evidence in litigation. A breach of compliance and security can be very costly to you and your business.

● Check that you understand the basic principles of the key five UK acts and any others specific to you and your business.

● Think before hitting 'Send' and ask yourself these three questions:

   1   To what extent might this email contravene the current legislation?

   2   Have I taken sufficient measures to limit a breach of confidentiality and security?

   3   If the email was used as evidence, what might be the cost to me (and my business) if the case went against me?

● Ensure your Acceptable Usage Policy is current, understood and accepted across the whole organisation, from receptionists to the CEO.

● While you require a clear email retention and destruction policy, you also need to be certain that the policy can be implemented. This generally means using appropriate technology to archive and destroy emails automatically.

● If in doubt about the legitimacy of an email, consult with legal experts before sending it.

CHAPTER 18

Protect yourself from an infection

Worms and viruses are increasingly being written to steal confidential data from innocent people's computers, to hijack resources, or launch spam or denial-of-service attacks.

Graham Cluley

The first computer virus (Elk Cloner) written nearly thirty years ago was relatively harmless and almost funny. Its intention was to display a poem every time your computer booted up. Today's cyber-crime is big business and often malicious. It comes in many forms, from viruses and phishing to spam. Emails and web downloads are the most common source of viruses. In this chapter we cover:

- the distinction between the three main sources of cyber-crime
- top tips to avoid being the target of a virus or phishing attack and reduce spam
- sources of further information.

Cyber-crime can be expensive. You will need to disinfect your computer if infected and you and your business may suffer reputational damage. Viruses are easily transmitted and others will become wary of email from you if your email image has been compromised. If you run a business, cyber-crime can result in a denial of service attack, whereby your website is temporarily shut down and everyone is denied access. If you use email for marketing, and do not take the necessary precautions, you can find your business email address is very quickly blacklisted.

 **tip**

Never open an email (or attachment) or follow a link in an email which looks suspicious (not authentic). Delete the email immediately.

Spam

Processing the estimated annual volume of 62 trillion spam emails is equivalent to driving around the world 1.6 million times.

'The Carbon Footprint of Email Spam Report', McAfee

In 2009 spam emails were estimated to account for 85 per cent of worldwide email traffic. The term 'spam' refers to unsolicited junk email and is often about how to enlarge your physical and financial status. The term is generally thought to have been derived from the 1970s *Monty Python* sketch on spam (you can see the original on YouTube). The alternative explanation is that it comes from the abundance of pink canned meat made in Britain after World War II. Known as Spam, it was one of the few items not rationed but not wanted.

There is a fine dividing line between having ferocious spam filters (which can also trap legitimate emails) and lax spam filters (which mean your email inbox is full of junk). Spam is costly in terms of the resources used to stop

spam is costly

it and time taken to trawl through spam filters to make sure nothing important has been accidentally trapped. It can take me up to 30 minutes a day to trawl through the spam emails.

Viruses

A virus is a piece of computer code which can harm your computer by infecting it and causing it to behave in unexpected ways. Viruses often mutate either through attachments or by opening your contact database and sending infected emails to everyone in there. A classic was the 'ILoveYou' virus in 2000. Contained in an email, it spread like wildfire and at least 10 per cent of businesses were hit. Since then, anti-virus software and surveillance has greatly improved.

Identity theft

This is a relatively new phenomenon. It is an attempt to steal your personal data (usually financial, such as bank details). There are two main sources of identity theft, phishing and key logging.

Phishing

The attack arrives as an email from what looks like a reputable source (for example, your bank, PayPal, HM Customs and Excise). You are asked to click on a website link to verify information which is then used to defraud you. Again this can be costly as institutions such as banks have now tightened up the terms under which they will reimburse you for such crimes.

Key logging

Attachments containing malware will install a piece of software on your PC which then records your every keystroke. (Malware is the term for any unpleasant software which may harm your PC and subsequently your personal identity.)

Cyber-crime as a major business threat

Although there are now many companies that specialise in detecting all forms of cyber-crime and providing anti-virus and spam software, the perpetrators of cyber-crime are becoming cleverer and more malicious by the day. Not surprisingly, the 2009 Davos World Economic Forum identified tackling cyber-crime as one of the top five challenges facing business.

 **tip**

Download and read 'Threatsaurus – the A–Z of Computer and Data Security Threats' from Sophos (www.sophos.com).

Out-of-office messages

Out-of-office messages can inadvertently open the backdoor to cyber-criminals and breaches of confidentiality. Such messages are now provided with most popular free email account providers (including Googlemail, Hotmail and Yahoo). The cyber-criminal does not distinguish between large corporate and individual email users. The risks related to using out-of-office messages apply equally to all users.

Limit the risk of a breach of confidentiality and burglary

Consider the out-of-office message below.

I am away on leave from 10 to 24 July. If your message is urgent, please contact one of the following. Jane Brown in connection with A. Fred Lane in connection with B. Will Bean in connection with C. Otherwise I will deal with your email on my return.

This is both unsafe and carries a high risk of breaching confidentiality. It would take a serious cyber-criminal only a few minutes to locate where you live and hence a possible empty house. Analysing the out-of-office responses to a recent e-briefing I sent revealed that 28 per cent of responses were insecure.

Giving three people as contacts and the projects/clients for whom they are responsible is also risky. You have now disclosed to possible predators (competitors, journalists, etc.) information you probably wanted to keep private. An example of a safe and secure out-of-office message is shown below:

I am out of the office from 10 to 24 July with limited access to email. If your email is urgent, please contact Jane Brown. Otherwise I will deal with the matter as soon as I can.

brilliant tip

When composing your out-of-office message, say only that you are away from the office. Give the name of one point of contact only and always check that they too are not on leave.

Some people give only a name (and maybe an email address) to deter unwanted people from phoning. They either make the assumption that key clients know who else to phone or they delegate access to their mailbox to another person.

Don't let the spammer in through the backdoor

Out-of-office messages can give away your email address to spammers. Spammers often generate random email addresses and, when they receive your message, they then know they have struck lucky.

On or off, which is the lesser of the two evils?

One charity that relies heavily on casual labour to man telephone helplines has suffered from pickpocketing through the use of out-of-office messages. A thief sent emails and, when he received people's out-of-office messages, he posed as these absent people to gain access to the building and steal.

Consider

For all these cyber-crime related reasons, many companies now ban the use of out-of-office messages for external emails.

✸ brilliant tip

Before deciding on your policy for use of out-of-office messages, weigh up the potential loss of business against the risks of cyber-crime, and then make a decision best suited to you (and your business).

Software tools to prevent cyber-crime

Today most email suppliers and businesses subscribe to one of the major anti-virus and spam services, such as Sophos and MessageLabs, which stop spam and viruses before they even enter your network. However, attacks can also be triggered by web downloads. Cyber-crime protection is therefore usually a multi-layered approach. Emails will be scanned at source before entering your business, on entry and, lastly, as they arrive at your computer.

Even if you are a sole trader, it is vital to have anti-virus/spam software on your computer/laptop in addition to that provided by your email supplier.

It is important to remember that anti-spam and virus software is reactive, not proactive, and can only be introduced once a virus, etc., has been spotted. Just occasionally it takes time for these to be spotted. A classic example is the 'Nigerian 914' scams whereby people are asked to give some money in order to release a much larger sum (for example, someone's estate). The growth of the internet led to a surge of these email scams in early 2000; however, although they still go on in various guises, today far fewer people are duped by them and they are more easily blocked by anti-spam software.

Unfortunately, deploying anti-cyber-crime technology is not sufficient. You also need to be personally vigilant about what comes unasked to your mailbox, especially spam.

Personal email management

Based on conversations with Graham Cluley of Sophos, here are some top tips to help you further protect yourself from being the victim of a cyber-attack. For more information and updates about the latest attacks, see www.brilliant-email.com.

To protect yourself from attack, **do** ...

- Update your anti-virus and security software daily. Sophos estimates that security researchers identify over 50,000 new sources of malware every day.
- Preferably pick a software solution that automatically updates itself.
- Make sure your anti-virus software scans all incoming email attachments.
- Keep alert and up to date about cyber-crime. Subscribe to at least one of the free email newsletters from the established reliable specialist companies such as Sophos and MessageLabs.
- Keep your main operating and applications software up to date (for example, Windows, Mac OS and Office).
- Review your sent items for emails sent but which you did not send – this is a sure sign that either you have a virus or your computer has been hacked.
- Use a different email address to your main account for subscribing to newsletters, chatrooms, etc.
- Construct a non-obvious email address of at least eight characters (for example, John56home@xmail.com).
- Be cautious about using out-of-office messages while away.

- Use your email software junk mail function to blacklist (block) potential spam emails which still creep through.

- Use 'Rules' to send potential spam automatically to the 'deleted' folder.

- Report persistent spam attacks to either your IT department or email providers.

- If they cannot stem the flow of spam and viruses, change your email name or email service supplier.

- Use proper email marketing software or a service provider (such as Constant Contact) if you do email marketing. This will protect your business email address from being blacklisted. See www.brilliant-email.com for more information.

To protect yourself from attack, **don't** ...

- Open unsolicited suspicious emails.

- Open/forward emails relating to a current crisis – for example, the death of a well-known celebrity or a natural crisis, such as an earthquake. Cyber-criminals use these events to perpetrate their wares and often send out fake emails, etc.

- Open/forward email alerts about viruses and spam as they are usually fake and the source of a virus/spam. If in doubt, go and check on one of the news sites mentioned below.

- Follow links in emails asking you to verify any form of information – these are usually phishing emails. Financial institutions such as PayPal do not normally send out such requests via email; they would phone. If you *do* think the email is genuine, don't follow the links in the email, type in the website address in the address line of your browser.

- Share your personal information online. As social networking increases, so too does the time cyber-criminals spend sniffing around these networks to detect where they can attack. Sophos estimate that 57 per cent of users of social networks have been spammed and 36 per cent have been sent malware via social networking sites.   *CHECK*

- Display your email address on websites such as your business website. This makes it easy for cyber-criminals to 'harvest' email addresses, which can then be spammed and used to send malware, etc.

- Use easy-to-guess email addresses. Spammers often use tools to automatically generate email addresses such as fred@, fred1@.

- Click on the 'Unsubscribe' link in with potential spam, as this just confirms your email address to the spammer. ✓

- Send bulk emails (i.e. to more than 30 people) straight from your personal email software. You will quickly find yourself perceived as a spammer.   *Check* *(?)*

Useful sources of further information

Here are some excellent sources of information, emails and newsfeeds to help you keep up to date on cyber-crime:

- www.sophos.com
- www.messagelabs.co.uk
- www.spamhaus.com
- www.moneysavingexpert.com (excellent for sources of free anti-spam and virus software).

☀ **brilliant** tip

To be alerted to current potential cyber-crime attacks, follow Graham Cluley on Twitter.

 recap

Cyber-crime is the bugbear of today's world of e-business. Attacks can be costly. Prevention is better than cure, which means you must invest resources to protect yourself. It is the last step in improving your productivity as a brilliant email user.

● Ensure your email provider uses good anti-spam and anti-virus software and make sure you put protective software on your own PC.

● Be diligent about which emails and attachments you open and links you follow.

● Keep abreast of emerging cyber-crime threats by subscribing to a good newsfeed/email newsletter.

● Update your anti-virus and anti-spam software on your PC daily (preferably choose software which automates this task).

● Ensure all your other application software is up to date.

● When on leave, use the out-of-office (auto-reply) message cautiously.

● See www.brilliant-email.com for more information and updates on the latest threats.

Summary: Keeping your mailbox under control

It is extremely difficult to teach grown-up people anything. It is, however, relatively easy to create conditions under which people will train themselves.

Sir John Harvey-Jones

This book has provided you with a wealth of tips and hints to help you deal with your mailbox more efficiently and improve your personal productivity. The key is to prioritise, prioritise and re-prioritise.

How will I remember all these tips?

One way that many clients find works well is to create an easy charter or code of best practice. Either I help them develop one specific to their business or they adopt one based on the charter I have created. Called the 'Nine Ps of Smart Email Management', this book is based on it.

For your own copy of the 'Nine Ps of Smart Email Management' send an email to information@brilliant-email.com with the subject line of 'Nine Ps checklist-EOM'.

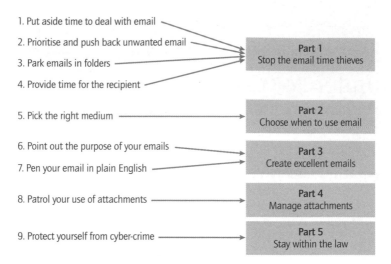

The Nine Ps of Smart Email Management

How much can I expect to gain from using email more effectively?

Does it work? People and organisations I have worked with quickly find themselves able to save time. How much depends on your starting point. Some of you may already be quite good at dealing with email and just need to top up your skills. Others starting at the bottom of the ladder can expect to save at least one hour a day.

How can I keep my mailbox under control?

Once you put all you have learnt into practice, you will notice your productivity increasing and that you have reclaimed your life from the mailbox. However, change does not happen overnight and it is easy to slip back into bad habits. Perhaps you will stop regular mailbox housekeeping and your emails may start to become sloppy. Projects, responsibilities and interests change. You will need to re-prioritise and re-look at some of the tips. Go back and look at sections you previously skipped over.

For reminders and more tips and hints you can also:

- Subscribe to my monthly ebriefing of tips and hints. Send an email to information@brilliant-email.com with the subject line of 'Add me to the ebriefing EOM'.
- Follow me on Twitter as the 'EmailDoctor' and/or become an 'EmailDoctor' fan on Facebook.

What about my colleagues?

However, all this will not stop your colleagues behaving badly with email. This includes internal and external colleagues, clients and prospects, advisers, etc. You will need to educate them too. This will enable you to sustain and make further productivity gains as shown below.

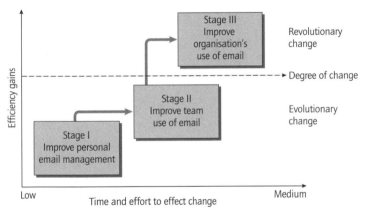

Benefits of changing email behaviour

Push back those emails you don't need and which fall short of being brilliant. Ask questions such as the following:

- What do you need from me?
- Why have you sent this to me?
- When do you need a response?

- Could we achieve our goals more quickly if we used an alternative to email?

- Does this email convey the right image for our business?

- Is there any way in which the content of this email might compromise us (leak confidential data, breach compliance, etc.)?

- How quickly can we find all the emails related to a project if needed?

- How much time can we *all save* if we all used email more effectively?

Start small by educating your inner circle. Then spread the word further afield. Several clients use either my 'Nine Ps of Smart Email Management' charter or one I developed for them and their trading partners and customers to help them all work more productively.

Is email here to stay?

As social media continues to infiltrate our lives, some commentators suggest we will soon see the death of email, especially because the younger generations seem tethered to Facebook and text messaging. Yet volumes of email are generally predicted to continue to rise by about 10 per cent year on year. (Part of this rise is due to more users expected to come online, especially from developing countries.)

In my opinion, we will see social networking becoming more dominant (both in business and socially) for ephemeral messages and general chit-chat. However, email will continue to be the dominant electronic communications medium (particularly for exchanges which may form part of an audit trail). Indeed, just look at how we receive status updates to our social media sites. A personal Twitter message even comes by email!

This book was written amid all the talk of entering an age of austerity. If there is one single area where time and money can be saved, it is in making email work for you and your business rather than letting it eat uninvited into your valuable time and resources.

For more resources go to www.brilliant-email.com. You can also email me with problems and your tips and hints (information@ brilliant-email.com).

Now go do some Brilliant Emailing. Good luck.

Further reading

Allen, David. 2001. *Getting Things Done*. London: Piakus.

Bamforth, Rob and Tarzey, Bob. 2008. 'Soaring not surfing'. Maidenhead: Quorcirca.

Barrett, Mary and Davidson, Marilyn. 2006. Editors, *Gender and Communication at Work*. Hampshire: Ashgate.

Direct Marketing Association. 2007. 'Direct Marketing Code of Practice 3rd Edition' and 'Email Marketing Council – Best Practice *Guidelines June 2007*'. London.

Egan, Marsha. 2009. *Inbox Detox*. Boston: Acanthus.

Ferriss, Timothy. 2008. *The 4-Hour Work Week*. London: Vermilion.

Freeman, John. 2009. *The Tyranny of E-mail*. New York: Scribner.

Giles, Jim. 22 June 2009. 'Email patterns can predict impending doom'. *New Scientist*.

Honoré, Carl. 2007. *In Praise of Slow*. London: Orion.

Jackson, Maggie. 2008. *The Erosion of Attention and the Coming Dark Age*. Prometheus Books.

Kellaway, Lucy. 2006. *Who Moved My BlackBerry?* London: Penguin.
——. 2010 *In Office Hours*. London: Fig Tree.

Mann, Merlin. http://inboxzero.com.

Mayer-Schönberger, Viktor. 2009. *Delete*. Oxford: Princeton University Press.

McGhee, Sally. 2005. *Take Back Your Life!* Redmond: Microsoft Press.

Mimecast. 2010. 'Email as part of a business continuity strategy'. London: Mimecast.

Osterman, Michael. 2009. 'A guide to document comparison and security for corporate legal.' Washington: Osterman Research.

PricewaterhouseCoopers. 'Information security breaches survey 2010'.

Seeley, Monica and Gerard Hargreaves. 2003. *Managing in the Email Office*. Oxford: Butterworth-Heinemann.

Sellen, Abigail J. and Harper, Richard R. R. 2002. *The Myth of the Paperless Office*. Cambridge, Mass: The MIT Press.

Shipley, David and Schwalbe, W. 2007. *Send*. Edinburgh: Conongate Books.

Spira, Jonathan B. and Goldes, David M. 2007. 'Information overload: we have met the enemy and he is us'. New York: Basex.

Tobleson, Paul, and Dunstan-Lee, Alex. 2007. 'e-disclosure: the 21st century legal challenge'. KPMG Forensic.

Truss, Lynne. 2003. *Eats Shoots and Leaves*. London: Profile Books.

Index

20 JULY — today

26 JULY — Sim's JHB witness

29 JULY   ENBLJHD
                ↓
              Greece   3 weeks.

work.

report.

USE "GH AWAY"
"In case of urgent, contact X on ___"

PARENT CONTRACT.
↳ parents to inform school of anything
change to child's life, death of
pet or relative, any domestic
discord, separation/divorce. etc.

Professionalism the corporate image/+ use

HCH Ltd. / Glendean.
This week's Sales (yipes!!)
      i.e. money in:

p. 133 email use

    STAFF HANDBOOK
    Never ⟶